Best Wishes

Order this book online at www.trafford.com/07-1425
or email orders@trafford.com

Most Trafford titles are also available at major online book retailers.

© Copyright 2007 Don Logan.

All rights reserved. No part of this publication may be reproduced, stored in a retrieval system, or transmitted, in any form or by any means, electronic, mechanical, photocopying, recording, or otherwise, without the written prior permission of the author.

Designed by: Don and Karen Logan

Note for Librarians: A cataloguing record for this book is available from Library and Archives Canada at www.collectionscanada.ca/amicus/index-e.html

Printed in Victoria, BC, Canada.

ISBN: 978-1-4251-3637-6

We at Trafford believe that it is the responsibility of us all, as both individuals and corporations, to make choices that are environmentally and socially sound. You, in turn, are supporting this responsible conduct each time you purchase a Trafford book, or make use of our publishing services. To find out how you are helping, please visit www.trafford.com/responsiblepublishing.html

Our mission is to efficiently provide the world's finest, most comprehensive book publishing service, enabling every author to experience success. To find out how to publish your book, your way, and have it available worldwide, visit us online at www.trafford.com/10510

 www.trafford.com

North America & international
toll-free: 1 888 232 4444 (USA & Canada)
phone: 250 383 6864 ♦ fax: 250 383 6804 ♦ email: info@trafford.com

The United Kingdom & Europe
phone: +44 (0)1865 722 113 ♦ local rate: 0845 230 9601
facsimile: +44 (0)1865 722 868 ♦ email: info.uk@trafford.com

10 9 8 7 6 5 4 3 2

TABLE OF CONTENTS

CHAPTER	PAGE NUMBER
MAP	2
INTRODUCTION AND ACKNOWLEGEMENTS	3
THE EARLY TRAIL	5
THE 1860'S	7
THE 1870'S	22
THE 1880'S	40
THE 1890'S	59
THE 1900'S	69
THE 1910'S	83
THE 1920'S	107
THE 1930'S	119
THE 1940'S	142
THE 1950'S	170
THE OLD SOURDOUGH (POEM)	178
INDEX #1	179
CONTRIBUTORS AND PHOTO CREDITS	184
INDEX #2	185
BIBLIOGRAPHY	186

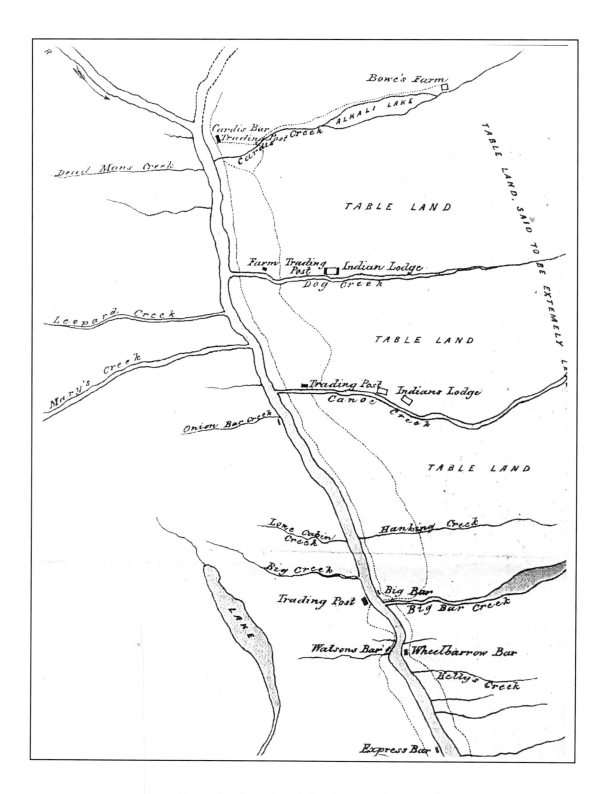

**Rough Sketch of the Cayoosh District.
Drawn by Corporal J. Conroy, Royal Engineer.
July 2nd 1861.**

INTRODUCTION AND ACKNOWLEGEMENTS

My interest in Dog Creek is a direct result of my hobby of exploring old historical sites with the goal in mind of recovering any overlooked artifacts or bottles.

It was in the early summer of 2005 when Mike Brundage of the Clinton Museum called to let me know that a gentleman from Dog Creek had been in telling him about exposing an old Chinese dump while laying some pipe. The next day Earl Cahill, local photographer and fellow explorer and I headed for Dog Creek. A few inquiries soon led us to Ted Hancock, the local bee keeper.

Well, soon after, in another fateful visit to the museum , Mike and I were discussing Dog Creek when a visitor from Williams Lake, Dorothy Unrau (nee Armes) spoke up and said that she had been born and raised there. It did not take very long to make arrangements to visit her and her mother, Doreen Armes and look at all their old photos. This was the beginning.

Many previous residents were most helpful with information and photographs but some are due special acknowledgement: Doreen Armes, who put her photo albums and written "Memory Journal" at my disposal, Betty Place who supplied me with a suitcase full of photos and newspaper clippings and Cariboo Chatelaine, the unpublished biography of Ada Place by A.J. Drinkell. Alfred Law, teacher in Dog Creek also needs to be thanked for his photographic documentation of life in the "Creek" , 1947-48, and his ongoing enthusiasm. Val Tranq for the history and photos of the Meason family. Last but not least special thanks must be given to Lyle and Mary James of the "James Cattle Company" and daughter Helen for their unlimited hospitality and access to their large ranch.

Trying to record everything that I had accumulated presented some problems, how to do it to make it presentable. My solution was to try and break it down chronologically and treat the decades of the first hundred years separately.

Needless to say the following leaves out many individuals. It would also be impossible to include all the photographs. A line had to be drawn somewhere and what follows is a summation of the information, photographs, and personal recollections that I have had the pleasure of accumulating during 2005 and 2006.

As a last word, all the prior residents I had the opportunity to meet had a keen interest in the history of the area as well as a nostalgic fondness for their time there. I sincerely hope the result was worth waiting for.

Most important is thanks to Karen for her assistance and unwavering support.

Dog Creek, 2006.

THE EARLY TRAIL

Although the original trail through Dog Creek has always been referred to as the "Fur Brigade Trail", it would have been used mostly by the indigenous people for local travel and trade. Branwen Patenaude in "Trails to Gold" refers to an 1862 essay in which the Hudson Bay packers had a favorite Chief at this location whom they called "Le Petit Chien". This would indicate that they dealt with or packed though Dog Creek, hauling goods and furs for the Hudson's Bay Co., prior to 1862. Dog Creek did not come into its own until after the B.C. interior opened up, a result of the discovery of gold.

The fur trail shows on an early survey map as coming off the mountain directly south of where the first grist mill was established. It wound across the south east corner of Yam Sing's lot no 12 G 1, down across Rabbit Park to the Creek. It was here at the crossing that some packer or miner built his log cabin which in later years came to be known as "The Dog Creek House", the center of what was to become "Dog Creek". From the valley the trail headed north following an esker to the plateau on Dog Creek Mountain and from there north to the goldfields.

The trail that enabled the miners to bypass the treacherous Fraser Canyon was started in 1858 by Governor Douglas. The Harrison route gave the miners what they referred to as the "River Route". This was to be improved upon from Lillooet north by the construction of the wagon road, begun in the spring of 1862. The new road turned North East after coming off Pavilion Mountain to arrive at Clinton thereby bypassing the trail north through Dog Creek.

Packer Jo Lindley published "Three years in the Cariboo", a record of his experience and observations as a packer in 1862. The route he describes north from Cayoosh Flat is that of the River Route. He describes the route from Pavilion to the next road house, as *"Now a low, soft trail crossing the Big Slide Creek to Leon's Station.* (Big Slide Creek is now Clinton Creek and the location of Leon's Station is today called Highbar). From Leon's to Canoe Creek Crossing, *"soft bad trail"*, from there to Dog Creek is *"now a very fair trail. Here the trail is near the river and then up along Alkali Lake to The Crossing"* (of Chimney Creek).

Packtrain, unpacking for the night.

Lindley writes *"Probably by this time the most hardy adventurer on the route is beginning to be well satisfied that it is no easy matter to get to the Cariboo, for though on paper I have not represented the trails to be very difficult of passage, you have doubtless found the Brigade Trail bad enough, and the River Trail, if you passed that way, just the worst of all trails that mortal man ever ought to think about getting over alive. Swamps and sloughs, hills, mountains, and along precipices until your head would swim; but no matter, we are now at Quesnel….not quite there yet".*

The River Route, particularly Dog Creek, had the advantage of feed for the pack animals that was not as readily available on the interior trail. Lindley states *"You cannot take a mule, pack him with "grub" tools and blankets, and start off on a two or three weeks' prospecting tour, as in California. The extreme roughness of the hill lands, and quagmire condition of the low country is so densely timbered that even grass cannot grow in sufficient abundance to maintain the animals, at the same time that it presents almost an impenetrable barrier to progress".*

THE 1860'S

Who was there first? No question, it was the natives, although representation was indeed sparse. Well then, who were the first non-natives? In 1861 Corporal James Conroy had drawn a sketch of the Fraser River from Foster's Bar in the south to the Chilcotin River in the north. Conroy was a Royal Engineer working for the B.C. government.

Dog creek is shown in detail on this map. Only three locations are indicated. The first and closest to the river is marked as "FARM". The second, just east of the trail was listed as "TRADING POST" and the third, further east, was marked "INDIAN LODGE".

The farm on the river was originally settled by Moise (Moses) Pigeon. Family history has Moses arriving in B.C. like most others of the time by following the Gold trail from California north to Canada. They would turn to farming, ranching and packing, realizing better returns than mining.

**Moses Pigeon
Born at Three Rivers, Quebec, October 6TH 1834.
Settled on what was later to be known as Lot #7 Group 6, Lillooet.
Today it is referred to as the "River Ranch"
Photo C-1874**

Samuel Leander Charles Brown was to become instrumental in the early opening up and settlement of the Dog Creek district. Charlie as he was known, was born in Kingston Ontario on December 23, 1826. He traveled to Santa Fe New Mexico where he established the first grist mill. News of "gold" was all he needed to set sail from Mexico to California in 1849. Unfortunately for Charlie, the boat he had picked met with disaster in San Francisco harbor. All passengers were saved, but Charlie lost everything, landing on the beach with only one boot.

Samuel Leander Charles Brown
C-1878

As Brown had mastered Spanish while in Mexico he soon got a job with good wages. He homesteaded a farm on the Sacramento River that he called "The Elk Horn Ranch". Once again news of "gold" in British Columbia instilled the wanderlust. He left the "Elk Horn" never to see it again.

Charlie left California with a pack train and packers heading overland to B.C. They traveled up the inland route, through the Okanagan and it was in the Similkameen valley that they encountered hostile natives. One of the packers was shot and killed and another wounded.

It did not take long for Charlie to realize there was more money to be made packing than searching for the elusive shiny metal. Many years later his son, James, would write that he classed him as "The best packer in B.C." James, in an article for the Bridge River-Lillooet News in 1938 would relate the following stories to substantiate his claim:

"On one occasion at the Fountain, a large gathering of miners took place. Men in those days were inclined to gamble and sport, and money was no object at the time.. There were arguments exchanged concerning a tank containing quick silver as to who could lift the tank with one hand on to a counter three feet high. Hundreds of dollars were wagered and scores tried and failed. No one ever dreamt that Charlie Brown as he was commonly called, who appeared to be a small man, possessed of any strength. However he made an effort and with crowning success lifted the tank on to the counter. Cheers and loud applause were rendered and the monies handed to the lucky winner.

Charlie continued packing until 1861 when he settled in Dog Creek and hired another to run his packing. James claimed in the article that not only was his dad the "Best Packer in B.C." he was in fact the "Best on the Pacific Coast".

"He packed all the machinery and boilers of the steamer "Enterprise" at Soda Creek. All other packers failed to accomplish the task. There were four billiard tables (eight miles north of Lillooet), which were to be transported to Barkerville. After several attempts among packers, they all failed. Mr. Brown was then asked if he could pack his animals with billiard tables, and remarked he could. He accomplished the task with no

difficulty – and received freight compensation of four thousand dollars in gold dust.
The tables were destined for the "Hotel de France" owned by French Bob and French Frank.

According to Frederick W. Laing, a noted B.C. historian, Brown located on and applied for 160 acres on Dog Creek on November 25, 1861. Brown never did complete the title on this piece and remained a squatter for some years.

It was about this time that Brown joined another settler in a new venture partnership. The partner was Conte de Versepeuch, Isadore Gaspard.

Conte de Versepuech, Isidore Gaspard?
This photo has been recently discovered behind a family portrait of his son Fred, by comparison with a photo of Isadore in much later years, I believe this to be Isidore.

He was born in St, Hippolyte, Aveyron, France in 1831, the son of Antoine and Ann Robert Versepuech.

Great grandson, Gordon Gaspard, wrote a brief family history in the First Nations publication "Secwepemc News" in June of 2002. He wrote *"According to legend, the Count Gaspard de Versepuech left his Paris home to replenish the family fortunes, first trying his luck in the California gold fields then in 1860 heading for Barkerville. Ending up at Dog Creek, the Count traded his elaborate tricornered hat and blue satin jacket worn at the Court of Louis XVI to Chilcotin chief Alexis for a tidy band of horses".*

In 1861 the partnership had Isadore making a special trip to San Francisco to purchase a set of French burr mill stones leaving Charlie in Dog Creek to erect the building for the first grist mill.

FIRST MILL ON MAINLAND
Here is a picture of the first flour mill to be built on the British Columbia mainland. It was built at Dog Creek in 1866 by Charles Brown.

Williams Lake Tribune 1958.
The date constructed should read 1861.

Isadore returned to Victoria, from San Francisco, on the 14th of April 1861. He had acquired a set of burr stones that had cost $175.00 and had purchased, in Victoria, a complete set of workings required to set up a sawmill, for $90.00. The stones he left in the customs house until the spring of 1862, when they were packed to Dog Creek via Douglas and Lillooet. However, he did bring with him 1000 pounds of wheat that he had purchased for 33 cent per pound. Although it was late in the season, they planted ten pounds to prove the crop would grow. In an article that Charlie's son Jim would write decades later, he said Isadore and Charlie had been ridiculed for thinking that wheat could thrive in the area. The following spring, 1862, the balance of the supply was seeded, resulting in a harvest of 12,000 pounds. Some of this was ground to flour in the new mill, some sold for seed to the other farmers at 23 cents per pound and the balance sowed the following year.

Painting of the original grist mill by Primrose Upton.

The sawmill was also up and running in 1862 but they found that the two could not be run profitably at the same time with the amount of water power available. Isadore would move the sawmill operation to his holdings approximately three miles up the creek from the grist mill. Jim Brown, in his article, said that the two entrepreneurs had incurred debts of $5500.00 during the construction. But that with good management and perseverance the debt was soon cleared up.

Grain soon became the major source of revenue for many of these new farmers. The following article appeared in the Cariboo Sentinel in 1862.

"It is a matter of the highest importance to the progress and development of this country that sufficient wheat and grain should be raised within its boundaries to supply its own consumption.

The amount of land this year under cultivation is unprecedentedly large and from the fact of the farmers having had several years experience in the country, we have no doubt the yield this year will approximate to the demand for next years consumption.

From Lillooet to Soda Creek, there is not a single ranch which possesses an acre of good farmland that the farmer has not engaged in its cultivation.

In the neighborhood of Lillooet alone upwards of 1,200 acres of wheat will be grown, and on the ranches at Williams Lake, a great deal of land has been laid down with the same crop....

Let us hope that the time is not far distant when flour instead of being 30 cents on Williams Creek will not exceed 10 cents."

By 1866 the wishes of the author of the proceeding article had materialized. On June 28th 1866, Peter Pullet of Clinton wrote the following article that appeared in the Cariboo Sentinel on the 19th of July,

"Dog Creek Valley....in which are located three ranches; the principal one is owned by Messrs Brown and Gaspard (Versepuche). Who possess a grist mill and a sawmill, the former of which has proved a great benefit, not alone of the neighboring settlers, but to the colony at large.... This mill, so far as my knowledge extends, was the first that was erected in the colony, at first it got a bad name for making poor flour, but the experience and further improvements remedied this, and from my own examination and use of bread made from the flour at different places, I can testify to its being now an excellent article."

F.W. Foster, storekeeper in Clinton, wrote ,

"Lillooet.... October 24th, 1866.... Flour is ruling here, extra brands $7.75 per 100, far cheaper than ever known before; all of it this season product.

About three hundred thousand pounds is on hand....it may not be generally known that the quantity of flour produced by the two mills at this town, and that at Dog Creek, on the Fraser will with very little help from the outside markets, be sufficient to support the wants of the whole upper country until what comes in again...."

By 1867 the small original burrs were no longer adequate for the volume of grain and a new set was ordered. Jim Brown stated that it was about this time that the partnership was dissolved. Isadore retreated to his property east of town and continued to farm and grow grain. Brown described him to be an *"excellent farmer"* and indicated that he was growing from 130,000 to 150,000 pounds of grain, which by that time was five to six cents a pound.

Charlie Brown continued to run the grist mill, store and hotel at the original site. In all probability the store and hotel would be the one shown on Conroy's map of 1861. (This would be substantiated by the original survey notes for the lot on which the grist mill stood. Only the mill and a smaller house were shown).

As these settlers were some of the earliest Whites to settle the interior there were no women of their own extraction to marry. It was only natural that they turned to the local natives for partners. The Hudson Bay Company would refer to these liaisons as "Country Wives", as often when "Whites" were available they would take a second more socially acceptable wife.
This was not the case with the men of Dog Creek as in most all the relationships, whether acknowledged by marriage or not, they remained long term.

Charlie Brown started his family with the birth of his son James Nathaniel Jerome Brown in 1864. His long term association was with a native woman Houpidsa. (The spelling of many Native and Chinese were up to the interpretation of the priest or official recording it and as it was based on the phonetic, many different spellings occurred for the same name). Charlie's second and third children, Charles and Henri were baptized in Dog Creek in 1867 & 1869 respectively.

**John Davis and Jim Brown,
two first generation decendants of the early Dog Creek settlers.**

Jesse Davis was another arrival in the sixties. He was English and listed himself as a farmer. John also took a native "wife" Takrwenack, who was the mother of five children with John. Both Mary and Martin Davis were baptized on November 13, 1867 in Dog Creek. It was in the Sixties that Davis applied for a pre-emption on 160 acres, the lot directly east of the grist mill. According to Branwen Patenaude in "Trails to Gold", Davis had been one of the original miners that had invested in the 29 Mile House on Pavilion Mountain. This venture was of short duration due to the high elevation and the availability of an alternate route, the Cariboo Road.

Isaac Davis on a highway
maintenance crew 1895.
Isaac was baptized in Dog Creek
July 16th, 1875.

Alfred Alexandre Davis
Alex, also, was baptized in Dog Creek
October 13th 1873.

Pierre Collin, another sixties arrival, was a immigrant from France. He also applied for an early pre-emption. His property was directly west of the wagon road and Oppenheimer's Hotel. It was to become lot # 6 group 6 Lillooet District. Pierre's native wife was Karnnatkwa (Anglicized to Catherine). They had two children who were baptized in Dog Creek, Pierre Junior on June 18th,1868 and Louis on June 21 1871.

A further portion of the Gaspard's article, by Gordon in June 2002 was as follows;

"The Count built the first sawmill in the area, where he built a pit and installed a whipsaw that ran from an overshot waterwheel mounted in the creek. From this sawmill he built a large house for his family and himself. He built a fireplace of adobe brick to warm the house in the winter.

He worked hard in his irrigated fields and grew hay, barley, oats, and wheat. Count Gaspard also had a small orchard of crab apple, currents, raspberries and rhubarb."

The Gaspard house as it looked in the late 1930's.

The Gaspard house was located on Lot #4 Group 6 Lillooet district. Isadore had made a down payment of $75.00 on October 9th, 1862 and the balance of $97.46 was paid on August 18th, 1871. The property was crown granted to him on December 18th, 1872.

Isadore married a native lady, Margaret Mootla, on June 16th 1882. On their wedding certificate Margaret's parents were listed as ;

Father- Kopmenak

Mother –Carmenaskat

Although they not were married until the 80's they already had a family of five children, the first born was Julia, in 1866. Matilda was second in 1870.

Matilda Gaspard.

There has always been some confusion as to what his name actually is. Isadore, himself, did nothing to help us in this regard. His parents on his wedding certificate are listed as "Versepuech", whereas he used "Gaspard" for his last name in the Census of 1881.

The Gaspard family.
C-1890

What was to eventually become lot #15 group 1, Little Dog Creek, was pre-empted in 1868 by Frederick Soues. Whether or not Fred actually lived on the site is unknown as the following year he transferred it to William Cargile.

Frederick W. Soues at his desk. He was the Government Agent and Gold Commissioner For Clinton for 34 years, from 1877 to 1911.

William Cargile retained the property until April 5th 1873 when W. L. Meason took over the pre-emption originally filed in 1868. The location was described as *"situated on the south side of Little Dog Creek, lying Southwest of the main trail now leading from Dog Creek to Alkali Lake"*.

Rafael Valenzuela was born in the state of Sonora Mexico to Francisco and Courision Margus Valenzuela in 1837. Exactly when he arrived in Dog Creek and built his wintering cabin is in dispute. Some historians have the date as 1860, after the gold rush started. A.J. Drinkell, a long time resident of the Dog Creek area, always considered the date to be 1856. This information was from Placida Valenzuela, Rafael's daughter, therefore he considered it to be first hand. Placida was born in 1863 in Port Douglas, B.C. (Placida listed it as Fort Douglas on her wedding certificate) her mother was a native named Annie. Placida married twice, first to the American, Bill Wright, who settled in Dog Creek on what became known as U.S. Meadows. The "U.S." was his brand. Her second marriage was to Marc Pigeon. Adding to the confusion of the arrival date, Placida had told Davey Anderson that she had arrived in Dog Creek as a little girl. This would make their arrival sometime after 1863. Davey Anderson's mother nursed Placida in her final years at Little Casey and Davey spent many hours listening to stories of the early years. She passed away at the age of 79 in Dog Creek.

The 1881 census shows 45 year old Raphael in the Williams lake-Canoe Creek area with the occupation of "packer", and head of the household living with a Chilean, Maria Ahzarez, aged 50.

At 48 Raphael married, on December 28, 1885, a native girl named Jeannie – alias Cheesi mat-iko, aged 17. Her father and mother were listed on the certificate as, "Indian man and woman". The wedding took place in Clinton.

Raphael and Jennie had a daughter Guadeloupe in 1888, she married Michael John O'Shea in Vancouver in 1918.

Another connection to Valenzuela was a wedding on Dec 16, 1889 between William Valenzuela (age 20) and Adelaid Peterson (age 15). The witnesses to the ceremony were R. Valenzuela and Billy. An easy supposition to make would be that William was a relative and possibly his son.

Another daughter, Francesca, was born to Raphael in 1884. She died of pneumonia at the age of 13. She had lived only 11 days longer than her father who also passed away of pneumonia on May, 29,1897 .

Dates of Interest: 1) Birth of William Laing Meason Jr. May 7th 1864.

In the 60's 2) Birth of Theresa Laing Meason, October 16th 1867.

3) Birth of Malcom Laing Meason, February 20th, 1869.

THE 1870'S

The sixties had seen miners and packers making the decision to settle down long term in Dog Creek. Five of these had applied during the 1860's for pre-emptions and purchase of land from the government. As a result, the government sent Edgar Dewdney in the summer of 1870 to make official the boundaries of these new lots.

Edgar Dewdney had received a degree in civil engineering in Devonshire, England and joined the B.C. Government service in 1859. His career took him across southern British Columbia where he was instrumental in the construction of a trail from Fort Hope to Rock Creek. This trail, sections of which can still be seen, bears his name "Dewdney Trail".

Edgar Dewdney 1865.

Page 32 of Dewdney's survey field notes are for "Mr. Harper pre-emption on Dog Creek Mountain, Lot 1 Group 6." This is followed on the next page with "Harper's purchase Lot 2 group 6, Dog Creek Mountain".

These two lots totaled 646.3 acres, slightly over one section.

Unfortunately Mr. Dewdney neglected to put an initial in front of "Harper" so that we are not entirely sure as to whom it was, Jerome or Thadeus. I tend to go with Jerome. These two lots were never taken up by Harper but were crown granted to Allan Graham. Lot 1, September 8th 1871 and lot 2, October 14th 1872. Lot 1 is still referred to "Harper's Meadow" and the creek running to the Fraser from Vert Lake is "Harpers Creek". Graham, was a 33 years old English immigrant when he purchased these lots, he would show up in Victoria in the 1881 census listed as "trader".

This cabin is located on Lot 1 and is locally called "Harper's Cabin", although it is not old enough to go back to the original pre-emption, it is very near the site of the original.

In 1870, Jerome was 44 years old. F.W. Laing in an article "Some Pioneers of the Cattle Industry" stated that *"Jerome Harper was stricken with a serious illness, and had to be taken to California, where he died four years later"*.

**Jerome Harper.
1865**

Jerome made his intentions clear in an ad published in the Cariboo Sentinel on Saturday December 23, 1871.   Under the column "New Advertisements" the following:

FOR SALE

The undersigned, wishing to retire from

Business.

OFFERS FOR SALE

The

CLINTON FLOURING and

SAW MILLS.

For particulars apply on the premises

Clinton B.C. Dec. 20, 1871   J.HARPER

Two small articles appeared in the newspaper concerning Jerome while in California. The San Francisco Bulletin wrote: *"Jan.24, 1873, Reports the insanity of Jerome Harper, of British Columbia. About a year ago, he took half a million of dollars in coin from Victoria to San Francisco, and the constant dread of parting with any of that large sum, has turned his brain. He has a brother in British Columbia, in business"*.

Jerome's obituary appeared in the Daily Standard December 10th, 1874.

" Death of Mr. Jerome Harper-Just before the steamer Los Angeles left San Francisco, word was received on board that Mr. Jerome Harper, the wealthy mill owner and stock raiser of Clinton, British Columbia, and brother of Mr. T. Harper, was dead, and found drowned in a bath tub. It has been ready known that he has been in failing health for some years past, and his reason had almost deserted him. He was living in Santa Barbara, at the moment of the sad occurrence".

The two lots surveyed by Dewdney for Harper eventually did end up as part of the Gang Ranch. Thadeus purchased them from Allan Graham at a later date and they were included in the package sale of the ranch in 1888.

Jim Brown described the early mail service to Dog Creek, *"The first mail carrier between Clinton and Dog Creek was an Indian. Sometimes the mail was carried on a pack horse, at other times the carrier snowshoed it with mail on his back. He was paid collectively by the Dog Creek settlers. This Indian, years afterward, would tell you with pride how he carried the mail on his back.*

In 1873 the first government-subsidized mail contract was let and the successful tenderer was John Gallagher, who carried the mail on a pack horse and a two horse toboggan-like sled in winter. This mail contract usually called for a term of four years".

This photo is from the Clinton Museum and is marked-Loading mail pack train, 1916.

1873 was the year that the government opened an official post office in Dog Creek.

William Walter Wycott was appointed the first postmaster. Wycott's vocation in the early years was that of "trader" and as there was only one hotel and trading post at the Creek in 1873, Wycott and the post office had to work out of Oppenheimer's. Born in Picton Ontario, he was the son of James and Mary Wycott. Like others he left home to follow the gold trail that for him ended in Dog Creek.

Wycott had a long term relationship with a local native girl, Matthilda (Maggie) Kwonsenak of Canoe Creek. A son Tom was born to them in 1869. However , Wycott did take a "city" wife . The same year that he was appointed postmaster he married twenty one year old, Annie C. Crang in Clinton. Annie was from Bude, Cornwall in England. This marriage would be short lived.

A child, Eva Frances was born on the 13th of September 1874 and Annie would die on the 26th of August, the following year, 1875. The cause, listed on her certificate, was "Congestion of the brain". It is unknown what happened to Eva as she does not show up with the Wycott family in any future records. (there is a possibility that they called her Maria, the 1881 census listed a Maria that would have been the right age, living in the Wycott household). Maggie Kwonsenak would once again become W.W.W.'s female of choice and was able to make him an honest man. William Walter Wycott would make it official and marry Maggie on May 4th 1903. He was 73 and she 55.

Wycott would eventually move across the river to lot #367 in Empire Valley. He pre-empted this lot in 1884, but was still listed in Dog Creek in the 1884-5 Directory. The flat below lot #367 has become known as Wycott Flats.

Harry Marriott, in his memoirs, told many tales of Wycott and his escapades. Harry tagged him with "Stranger Wycott" due to his habit of addressing everyone he met as "stranger".

Ernie Thoresen in his "Memories of the Cariboo, wrote:

"Another character whom I met at the Gang Ranch was an old settler by the name of Bill Wycott. He had come into the Cariboo in the early days and had been to Kamloops when it was a Hudson's Bay trading post in 1870. He had a ranch west of the Gang ranch and at one time had quite a few cattle. In later years, owing to his age, he just let his cattle run wild. His means of transportation consisted of a gray horse and a two wheel

cart. He would make trips as far as Ashcroft and anything he saw that he could pick up he would load it on his cart. A story I heard at the Gang Ranch- A man dreamed that he went to heaven and knocked on the pearly gates. St. Peter came to the door. The man says "Can I come in?" St. Peter said "I can't unlock the gate old Bill Wycott was here and stole the keys".

Thoresen went on to tell of another occasion of meeting Wycott:

"One night Bill Wycott came to the ranch with his grandson Tom. Had supper at the ranch and then visited us in the bunkhouse. Old Wycott spoke up and said "Have any of you boys got an extra blanket you could loan an old man, the nites are getting chilly"?

No one gave him a blanket. About 9:30 Charley Morrow, bronc buster, went out to the barn to check on some horses, when he came back with a big grin, said "Hell, the old man and his grandson are asleep in the haymow and they have five or six blankets under and over them"!

These two photos are of the Wycott homestead, house and barn, Lot 367, Empire Valley.

William Laing Meason

William Laing Meason was born December 28th 1822 on Scotland's Orkney Islands. When he was twenty years old he joined the British Army as an Ensign in the 60th Rifles. He later transferred to the 71st Light Infantry where his rank was Lieutenant. The army was his life until 1850 when he sold his commission and emigrated to North America.

He was regularly described as a Greek Scholar. Educated in Scotland and Italy, he was as his obituary would describe: *"A linguist of no mean ability, being well versed in French, Spanish and Latin languages".*

Meason arrived in California and worked his way north through Washington Territory to arrive in Lillooet in 1859, the beginning of the Gold Mining "hay days" in the Cariboo. He became a packer.

In May of 1867 Meason purchased two hundred acres of land in Williams Lake, but his permanent home was to be Lesser Dog Creek. It was here that he took over the title of what was to become lot #15 G 6 Lillooet District. By the time of his death in 1905, he had acquired about eleven hundred and fifty acres that were crown granted.

**Meason's Little Dog Creek Ranch.
C-1920's.**

April 7th 1876 Meason was appointed Justice of the Peace for Cariboo and Lillooet District. He was also appointed to act as Indian Agent for Williams Lake, a position he would hold until 1894.

At the time of his death in 1905 Meason had four sons, William Jr. Malcolm, Magnus, and Gilbert and four surviving daughters, Celestine, Eleanor, Theresa and Annie. A fifth daughter, Mary died at the age of twenty.

Henri Otto Bowe and wife Theresa (nee-Meason)

Meason left the ranch and all his cash to his three sons, Gilbert, Magnus and Malcolm. There was to be a cash settlement of $250.00, payable in five annual installments of $50.00 to his fourth son William Laing Junior.

There would also be the stipulation to the three boys that they continue to supply a home for their mother and three sisters as long as they remained single. Theresa had married Henri Otto Bowe in 1885. The unmarried girls remained at home for some time as Eleanor and Celestine would marry in 1913 but Annie not until 1918. Meason may have thought Gilbert not responsible enough as he had put in the stipulation that he could not dispose of his share until he was twenty five years old.

A marble headstone is today, still maintained, on the original site.

Jack and Eleanor (nee -Meason) McLuckie.

Annie Meason..

Three photos from the Meason Family collection.

Fred and Celestine Rose (nee Meason)

Meason cattle roundup at Dog Creek.

With the sale of lot #15 to William Meason, William Cargile would move with his family and open a saloon and trading post on what is today lot #11 in Dog Creek. The building was directly east of the Oppenheimer trading post and neither was legally registered. This site would end up in litigation at the end of the decade. Cargile then moved to Clinton where he showed up on the 1884-85 Clinton directory as a trader situated in Clinton.

The present day "Hat Creek House" would be the next home for the Cargile family. In 1955 the Geographical Naming department for British Columbia adopted the geographical name for Hat Creek House as "Carquile". This would be rescinded on January 15th 1987.

The Kamloops Museum, in 1978, would have the following for "Place Names of the Kamloops District": *"Cargile is sometimes erroneously rendered Carquile. In 1881 William Cargyle, earlier of Dog Creek, bought a ranch and ran a good road –house, which still survives"*.

The "Rush" was beginning to slow after the initial onslaught of the miners who gleaned the easy pickings along the Fraser and the tributary creeks. This would bring in what would be considered as the clean up crews, the Chinese.

The Chinese had been following the "49ers" north from California, they were more patient and industrious than the whites and were prepared to expend much more effort in the recovery of the precious metal in exchange for a much smaller return.

The first reference to the Chinese in Dog Creek was the application for a pre-emption of 320 acres on October 4th 1876. The applicant was Yam Sing. I shall refer to him as Yam Sing although the census lists him as Lum Sing and another directory lists him as Ah Sing. As I discussed earlier, this is an example of the interpretation of the phonetic spelling. Yam Sing was born in China in 1841. His occupation on the census was listed as storekeeper.

Yam Sing built a hotel and trading post here, dedicated mostly to the supply and entertainment of the Chinese miners located in Dog Creek. This hotel became known to the locals as "The White House". My many trips to the site would uncover remnants of their gambling and entertainment.

A selection of larger liquor bottles found at the site of the "White House". The pear shaped bottle just left of center is what is commonly called a "Tiger Whiskey". It is a Chinese rice wine that was 48% alcohol. It was generally imported under the guise of medicine. I have one with the label still attached and the recommended dose was *"For Chinese only-Two tablespoons with each meal every day"*.

There were no leisure activities for the Chinese bachelors to indulge in other than alcohol, gambling and the dulling of senses with a dose of opium. The site would relinquish many hundreds of what we call opium bottles. Whether they contained opium or a powdered derivative is not known. One that I have uncovered at the site still has its original red powder.

Opium containers were also abundant. The opium came in small tin containers and they had a tiny incised Chinese character on the lid.

The Clinton Museum has in its files copies of articles that John R. Tait, a long time resident, published in the Ashcroft Journal. In the following excerpt Tait described the use of the drug;

"There is the case of Charlie Soues…..I remember him quite well from when I was a young boy….I got so acquainted with him, that I would sometimes, when going by near his shack, call in to visit him. He smoked opium. When he used it he would be on his bunk with a bamboo pipe pole which was a foot or more long with a bowl on the side of it with a cover that had a hole in the centre. There was an oil light by the bunk. He had a wire, like a knitting needle, which he would dip into a jar of opium, hold it to the light and draw the opium smoke into his mouth and lungs. I got so interested in this procedure that I tried it out at two different times but only the twice or I might have followed Charlie who hanged himself at Suicide Gulch".

Some of the smaller artifacts from the White House, opium and medicine bottles, coins, buttons, buckles, dominoes, "Go" buttons, a shot glass etc.

Gordon Armes and sister Dorothy Unrau, July 29th 2005.
Enthusiastic riders, they were with the "Cariboo Ride" that had stopped for lunch at the site of the old hotel, where I was digging. Both Gordon and Dorothy were born and raised in Dog Creek.

Yam Sing's coins. They date from 1863 to 1902. The small one, center bottom, is a "One Mil" minted in Hong Kong in 1863 and would buy a bowl of noodles and a steamed bun. It was 1/100th of a penny.

A very detailed description of Yam Sing's lot was included in the survey note;

"Survey of 160 acres for "Yam Sing" a Chinaman, date of record Oct. 4th 1876. Situated on Dog Creek-320 acres recorded but only 160 surveyed, the Chinaman did not wish to get anymore, being all mountainous & valueless. A stand for a store and a small garden is all the ground he needed. The 160 acres consists of steep mountain side with scattered timber, a few springs and some grass, but not an acre of cultivable land".

NOTE OF INTEREST- In 1870, when Dewdney surveyed the lot for Jesse Davis, (#5) he made note that the land directly east was designated as "reserve".

A typical Chinese Coolie crew, such as worked for Yam Sing.

The 1880's

The summer of 1880 brought B.C. Land Surveyor John Jane to Dog Creek at the request of the following settlers who wanted to legitimize their holdings;

Thomas and Isaac Saul had pre-empted lot #13 and 14, located between Dog Creek and Little Dog Creek. Thomas was 47 years old and had immigrated from County Wichton, Ireland.

I don't believe they lived on site, but used it for winter grazing for their pack animals. Thomas was a packer and was listed in the upcoming census as mail carrier. His location at the time of the census was the household right next to the Gaspard family. Lots 13 and 14 are known today as "Saul Field'.

Anthony Twentyman, a miller, was born in Cumberland England. Although Twentyman did not ask for a survey of his property, he was the beneficiary of having a small area between lots 5, 6 and 11, that had been or were being surveyed at the time. Jane, the surveyor, wrote on his field notes:

"Survey of a plot of cultivated ground belonging to a flour mill, this land has never been recorded in anyway, but I have surveyed it so as to include the buildings and fenced land. The property formerly belonged to Charles Brown but is now owned by Mr. Twentyman. Area about 8 acres as per sketch".

The sketch showed the mill and house adjacent. This eight acre parcel would not be registered until Frank Place pre-empted lot 2288 on May 17th 1911.

Mr. Twentyman continued to run the mill until he was hurt in an unfortunate accident . He was kicked by a horse on September 7th 1891 and died on the 13,th aged fifty five.

John Gallagher was born in County Donegal, Ireland in January 1827. Gallagher had been successful in acquiring the first mail delivery contract to Dog Creek. It had been awarded in 1873 and was a four year contract. This would be followed by his appointment as the replacement postmaster for W. W. Wycott in 1876.

January 24th 1876 Gallagher recorded a pre-emption on Lot #11 for 320 acres. This was the site where Oppenheimer's store and Cargile's saloon were located. In the very near future the Oppenheimer's store would become the famous "Dog Creek Hotel". Gallagher must have made some agreement with the Oppenheimers for the trading post as he would be free granted the lot on March 9th 1881, for the grand sum of $5.00.

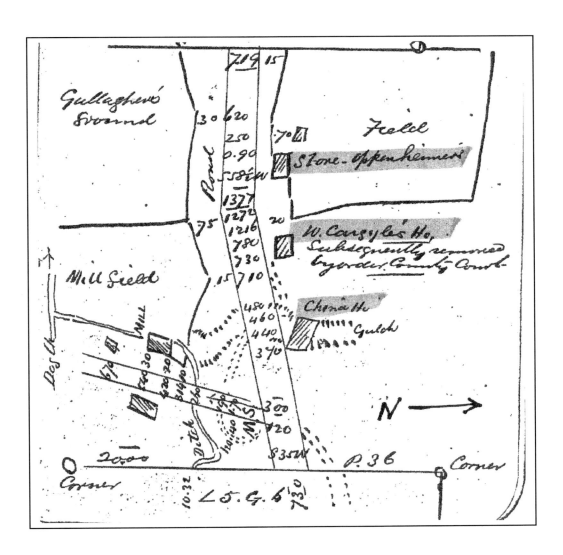

John Jane's sketch of Dog Creek survey of 1880.

The previous sketch from the field notes of Jane is very informative as to the location and ownership of the buildings and land that were at the time downtown Dog Creek.

Three of the buildings were located on the north side of the wagon Road, the trading post was marked as "*store-Oppenheimers*". Directly east was the Cargile place with the notation "*Subsequently removed by order County Clerk*". The third was a Chinese house across the wagon road from the grist mill.

On the south side of the wagon road there was only the grist mill and the accompanying house.

The value of Lot # 11, Gallagher's pre-emption, was in the trading post and store. The land was described by Jane:

"*Note-*

There is a little good land near the creek, say 10 acres in all, that could be cultivated, the rest consists of stony foothills, fit only for grazing; the claim is valuable as a site for a store-Oppenheimers of Yale have had a branch business here for years".

The Oppenheimer household in Yale was run by Isaac: a large household of seven family members and a support staff of six , an accountant, four clerks and a Chinese cook.

Note of interest:

1) On a baptismal certificate dated September 27th 1876, in Dog Creek, John Gallagher was listed as father. The mother was Mathilde Kounshenac, long term country wife of William W. Wycott.

Nancy Gallagher would be raised by the Wycotts. She shows up in the Wycott household as a domestic in the 1901 census.

2) April 4th 1881 was the official date for the Canadian Census. William Laing Meason was the enumerator.

The census shows the population mix for Dog creek to be about fifty Caucasian and thirty six Chinese. Natives were not enumerated until the 1901 census. The one exception was Meason's own wife, who's ethnic heritage he listed as "indigenous". No other native wives were listed. The ratio of Whites to Chinese soon changed to a more even mix as the Boyles, Wycotts and Browns crossed the river to settle in the Empire Valley and the Cargiles left for Clinton and Hat Creek.

As the enumeration was conducted and numbered from one household to the next, it is quite easy to conclude where some of the people were living at the time. For instance, the Cargiles were living in the house marked on Jane's field notes. In the census the next household included John Gallagher, Nils Gustafson and Dan Angus. This would have been at the Oppenheimer store and post office. The household next to Anthony Twentyman's and Charlie Brown's was that of Mr. And Mrs. Low Ah (the only Chinese woman in Dog Creek), Chun Ah, Chong Ah (miner), and Tack Ah. This would be the building marked "Chinese House" on Jane's sketch.

The three households listed before that of Yam Sing's contained twenty six Chinese, ranging in age from 24 to 43 years. These were, with one exception, all miners. The exception was Moi Ah, farmer (he possibly looked after Yam's garden). I have been told of three cabins on the west side of the road on Yam's lot and these would probably have been their living quarters.

There is a distinct possibility that these bachelors would have been indentured to Yam Sing. As the Head Tax did not start until 1885, all Yam would have had to pay for them to come to Canada, would be their fares from China. This advance would be repaid over many years.

Lot # 11, the store site, was crown granted to John Gallagher on March 9th 1881, but financial hardship plagued Gallagher throughout the summer.

George Byrues, the Sheriff of Cariboo and Lillooet Districts, was to sell Gallagher's holdings by public auction on the 21st of June 1881. The sale was to satisfy the judgement of F.W. Foster, a businessman and store keeper, in Clinton, B.C.

Byrues wrote:

"...the lands hereafter described were sold by me at public auction at Clinton, B.C. on the 21st day of June 1881, to Rafael Valenzuela for the sum of six hundred and seventy five dollars....".

Valenzuela ran the store and hotel until the summer of 1886. I believe that this is where the misconception that Valenzuela built the original store became accepted history. I contend that he was the owner who built the hotel addition to the original store.

The Dog Creek Hotel and Store c -1880's.

Rafael sold his interest to Joseph Smith Place. The following is a copy of the hand written conveyance that covered the sale:

"Dog Creek B.C."

"For and in consideration of the sum of $1890.00 Eighteen hundred and ninety dollars, I Rafael Valenzuela, of Dog Creek in Lillooet District, have this the 26th day of July 1886 Bargained and sold to J.S. Place of Nicomen in Yale District, all my right and title to 320 acres of land situated in Lillooet District known as Lot 11, Group 1, on Dog Creek together with all improvements thereon, consisting of Hotel & Store together with

all store stock, all fencing, crop, chickens together with all other appurtenances. Receiving for such $1300.00- thirteen hundred dollars down in cash payment for delivery of 7336 lbs. of freight from Nicomen to Dog Creek included therein the rest amounting to $590.00 five hundred and ninety dollars to be paid at his, J.S. Place's own convenience.

One piece of land 75 front by 100 feet back, being reserved, it being sold to a Chinaman by name of Ah Lee".

The above transaction is the first record of the Hotel in Dog Creek.

Joseph Smith Place.

Note of Interest:

1) As indicated earlier, The reserve was designated as early as 1870. Shown on Dewdney's field note, the reserve was surveyed by Jennett on September 15, 1883. It was an area of 357.5 acres and allotted officially by Commissioner Riley on July 19, 1884 as Dog Creek Reserve #1.

2) Until the early 1880's the only route north from Dog Creek was by the pack trail. John Janes survey map of 1880 shows a dotted line north from the hotel around the Dog Creek Mountain escarpment. It was marked as *"Course of new wagon road around mountain"*.

The availability of liquor in Dog Creek created problems for William Laing Meason the Justice of the Peace. He wrote to Frederick Soues, Government Agent in Clinton, the following letter on November 18th 1881:

"Sir-

I have the honor to inform you that for the preservation of the Peace, it is necessary either-

To stop liquor licenses on Dog Creek or to appoint a permanently paid Constable for that settlement.

To say nothing of the Crimes that frequently occur, like the one just tried by me at the assizes-The Indians procure <u>*all the liquor that they can pay for,*</u> *and the parties holding the licenses are unable or unwilling to help to discover the culprits.*

Some Indians obtain as much as two or three bottles at once, and taking the supply to their rancheries, scenes of howling drunkeness there take place which are the terror of the sober and peaceful members of the tribes.

One Indian was drowned in swimming across Fraser river when <u>*drunk.*</u>

Another broke into the house of F. Chelsea to assault him. <u>*Drunk.*</u> *This last you will hear of soon.*

Besides many other cases of Indians drunk and disorderly that would be too numerous to mention.

It is the constant customary habit at Dog Creek to gamble publicly with the Indians in the bar rooms and even Band Ring games are there and there played…."

Meason goes on to cite the "Statutes of Canada" in detail to explain his inability to control the situation.

"The revenue derived from the liquor licenses of Dog Creek is $120.00 per annum.

This one case Twentyman and Montgomery will cost the Country nearly $300.00.

The Indians are now so accustomed to liquor and know so well how and where to procure it-that as long as liquor is sold on Dog Creek they are certain to obtain-as they now do-all they are able to pay for.

As for Information – no one will give it.

Finally I assure you that unless the supply of liquor is stopped on Dog Creek some serious crimes will be perpetrated by the Indians in their drunken orgies.

Hoping therefore that you will seriously consider my request before issuing liquor licenses for 1882".

There is no indication that Meason's recommendations were ever implemented. Liquor continued to be sold and a full time Constable was not appointed.

Natives continued to be the cause of concern to the local settlers.

On March 19th 1883, a group of notable settlers in the Chilcotin wrote the following letter to Lieut. Col. Powell, Indian Superintendent, Victoria:

"We inhabitants of Chilcotin beg your attention with regard to the Indians resident here. There is existing a state of lawlessness among them that makes it all but impossible for us to remain in our places, owing to their depredations.

All here have treated them always with justice and fairness, frequently too, with much generosity assisting them in their needs, and giving them often seeds to use; but have been requited by ingratitude from most of them.

Some years ago on the occasion of their killing a number of cattle, we had three of them arrested and they were committed after trial before W.L. Meason, J.P. Others were guilty also, and evidence to that effect would have been obtained, but through carelessness of the Keepers at Clinton those committed were permitted to escape, stealing and taking Goat blankets with them in their flight. Since then we have endeavored to get along the best we could with them, though satisfied that some of them were still persisting in their depredations.

The season now past they have been carrying their violations of all law with increased boldness. According to the testimony of some of them they have killed seven head of cattle of Mr. Harper, eleven of Withrow & Fields, and of the rest of us, as yet an unknown number, but undoubtedly, a proportionate number.

Other offences have been done by them, as stealing and housebreaking, for which some of them have been arrested and committed for trial.

Among which are two sons of one of the Chiefs (Toosie) here, and doubtless he was fully aware, and most probably shared in the proceeds of these depredations.

We submit that if not convicted he be deposed from his Chieftainship, for it is unnecessary to state how much his example must influence, for evil, the rest.

For nigh eleven years now a Chilcotin has been running at large who murdered a Chinaman opposite Dog Creek. Then too, some of those now in jail and others as yet at large have vowed they will kill those informing and those concerned in their arrest.

We submit that matters have reached such a crisis as demands energetic and prompt action, and that we be not living here, as it were at their sufferance. Prompt action taken in regard to them may prevent more serious consequences".

> *L.W. Riske*
>
> *Samuel Withrow*
>
> *Silas Fields*
>
> *Benjamin F. English*
>
> *Donald McIntyre*

The response from the Indian office in Victoria was one of concern but passed the problem on to the local J.P. for solution, as these crimes were under his jurisdiction. He sent a copy of his response to W.L. Meason.

In addition to the murder of the Chinaman mentioned in the previous letter, Meason convened a Coroners Inquest for the murder of two Chinese on the west side of the Fraser River near little Dog Creek. The inquest was held at Dog Creek on April 19th 1883. The official details are :

"Proceedings of a Coroner's Inquest convened by the authority of W.L. Meason J.P. to ascertain the cause of their death of two Chinamen, Pack Sing &Chung Hang found dead in their cabin on the bank of Fraser River on the west side about 1 ¼ miles below Ah Packs ranch on said river, the jury having been sworn by W.L. Meason J.P. at Little Dog Creek and John E. Moore Esq. having been chosen foreman and sworn as such proceeded to view the bodies and report as follows;

One of the Chinamen, Pack Sing was lying on his bed, as if shot when sleeping the ball went in under the left shoulder and came out at the right…. The other Chung Hang was lying on the floor, the bullet entered his forehead….

The Chinaman who escaped states, "Two Indians came to our cabin Friday evening April 13th and got their supper. They went away and came back in the morning early when we were still in bed and shot the first one, Pack Sing. The second one Chung Hang then jumped out of bed and looked up at the hole from where the shot had come, and said what are you doing or something of that kind, when the Indians shot him. One of the Indians was lame and used a stick to walk. The other was a little shorter in size. We examined the ground round the cabin and found marks of a stick as if used by a man leaning his weight on it…. On the roof of the cabin we found marks of the stick and moccasins marks at the place where the shooting must have been done. The hole in the roof is about 20x16 inches. The Chinaman who escaped states also," I got into a corner of my bunk, the upper one, and the Indians shot twice at me but did not hit me". We found that from the hole in the roof a weapon could not be aimed at the place the Chinaman showed us that he was in. The Chinaman who escaped also states that after the others were killed, he found that the door had been tied on the outside.

We found that dirt had been scratched down from the roof on the inside where the surviving Chinaman said he had been trying to make the hole larger to escape through but that he heard or thought he heard the Indians outside so he ceased his work. The Chinaman also states that the two Indians when they came to the house were riding two horses, one of a red colour , the other grey or white....".

John Moore, the foreman at the inquest, with daughter Dilly and Aggie Pigeon, in New Westminster, B.C..

It did not take long for the culprits to be apprehended. A telegram dated May 5th 1883 from Soda Creek announced that Doc English, Boswell and the Indians had captured the murderers. However, English had got the Indians to turn in the suspects by promising one hundred cases (telegram did not say what) and promising on behalf of the Government to release the Indians at Cariboo. He proposed to release them on bail if they were not prosecuted.

They were released "on recognizance" in the amount of $200.00 each on May 9th 1883. They were to appear at Clinton on the seventh of June. Sorry, can't tell you the outcome.

On August 30th 1884, Meason wrote to a close friend, Thomas Elwyn of Lesser Dog Creek. In this letter he tells Elwyn that Moses Pigeon has been detaining him for two hours, advising him of his impending marriage. Meason makes very clear his opinion on the wisdom and sanity of a 53 year old marrying a child of 14. He wrote this example : " *Field who is somewhere between 60 and 70 - & old at that, is going to marry a daughter of Dunlevy's age 13-14.... There should be some law to prevent this awful state of affairs*".

Meason's opinion aside, Moise (Moses) married Theresa Simone of Alkali Lake on September 16th 1884. He was 48 and she was 15.

Moses was obviously successful in his profession. He was listed as "cattle raiser" and he very soon after marriage built his family a home to be envied.

The Pigeon's "Grandview Ranch House".

Notes of Interest:

1) The wedding registration shows Theresa's father as Philipi Simoni and mother as Indian Stupinfa. Moses' parents were listed as Pierre Pigeon and Louise Lacroise.

2) John Gallager was appointed Justice of the Peace for Big Bar Creek on December 27th 1883.

3) Birth of Gilbert Meason, February 24th 1884

4) 1885 - James Nathaniel Jerome Brown publishes "The Rural Backwoodsman" the first paper in Lillooet along with a book of verse, "Western Fragments".

Pigeon Family Portrait.

Percy,

Moses,

Peter,

Claude,

Louie, &

Theresa.

The lot that Moses had settled on at the river was too small for his new family and his cattle ranch. He applied for land approximately twelve miles east of the Dog Creek Hotel. This was the beginning of the "Grandview Ranch" or as it's also known the "Pigeon Ranch". Lots #84,85,86,87 were surveyed for Moses on October 20th, 1885.

The children born to Theresa and Moses during the 1880's were:

Peter Moses, born June 5th 1886.

Claude, born January 4th 1888.

Granddaughter Patricia Riley recalls the enchantment of the large house at Christmas:

"A family Christmas gathering in a large, white country style home with a porch which was in the front and all on one side.

Christmas Eve found the family gathered in front of a large tree with Grandma sitting in the middle surrounded by the family. All hell broke out when Santa arrived and as he bent to kiss Grandma on the cheek she said "Why you dirty old thing" which didn't go over too well and Mother had to take me out of the room and explain that Santa was a very good friend who everyone knew, Tom Cooney. Of course I did not realize that the males had been in the barn having a little bit of cheer and it was his whiskey breath that she took exception to and not Santa. I don't think they would have dared bring a bottle into the house".

More of Pat's memory of the big white house:

"The upstairs of the two story house was a large attic filled with all kinds of odds and ends which would certainly now be antiques. One fascination was a Victrola complete with large hearing horn. The records were dark brown and about ¼ inch deep. Of course we were not allowed to touch…. Another place we spent much time was in a big long doorless shed connected to the barn which was filled with fancy cutters with red velvet type seats and resembled one like Santa would have arrived in. Others had shiny black seats and all were definitely of an era long gone".

Grandview Ranch

Clockwise from top,
winter at the main house, haying piles and stooks,
the barn, coming home at the end of day.

Pat Riley was still living at the Riley Ranch at Big Bar when this house burned down. Pat states: *"Aunt Aggie and Grandma were the only ones there as Uncle Ray was out riding on a beautiful fall day. Very little was saved and I don't think Grandma ever got over the horrendous experience of seeing her entire life go up in smoke. They were forced to make a home out of a two story log building that was always used to store food staples, i.e. dried fruits, which was all one smelled when entering the place".*

**The storage building the family moved into after the fire,
as it was the summer of 2006.**

Note of interest:

1) Named for the Pigeon family, the geographical feature Pigeon Creek, runs into Dog Creek at the Pigeon lot #87.

2) Joseph S. Place was appointed postmaster in October 1886, a position he would hold until May of 1924.

Nils Gustafson was a young Swede, twenty fours years old at the time of the census in 1881. When Moses Pigeon took his new bride to the Grandview Ranch he sold his River Ranch to Nils. This he continued to run until approximately 1920. He also applied for land at the headwaters of Dog Creek. Lot #114 was surveyed for him by W. Allan on November 22nd 1887.

Nils married Sarah Ann Manly in the Clinton District on November 28th 1899.

**Like many other ranchers starting out, Nils would work on road crews to subsidize his income.
Pete Gagne, Joe Truan, Louis Jarvis, John Cunningham, Ken Cunningham, Nils Gustafson, Napoleon Fisset, Bud Truan.**

By 1901 he had become a successful and substantial cattle rancher. The Empire Valley Ranch ledger for the summer of 1901 shows the sale of 253 head of cattle to Nils.

The lakes Gustafson and Neilson were named for the Gustafsons. The location and ownership of lot #114 became an issue during the summer of 1995. The "Gustafson Lake Stand-off" as it was to become known, was eventually settled but with much hype and media coverage. To the natives this land was known as "The Sundance Grounds" and considered sacred.

Note of interest:

1) Fourteen year old William Mason Brown (Son of Charlie Brown) died at the Empire Valley Ranch on the 26th of August 1888. He died of diarrhea after only one day sickness.

2) Thaddeus Harper's Gang Ranch experienced financial difficulties during the 1880's. In December of 1888 the B.C. Land and Investment Co. agreed to the appointment of a receiver. The B.C.L.&I. Co. would have their offer of $225,000.00 accepted for Harper's Gang in August 1889.

Joseph Smith Place was born in Bury, Lancashire, England January 24th 1854. He came to Dog Creek from the Nicomen House on the Thompson River, just north of Lytton.

Hilary Place in his book "Dog Creek, A Place in the Cariboo" wrote that his grandfather had married Alice Coxon, daughter of the road house owner, and had two children George and Alice. When his wife Alice died, her mother took the two children south to California. Soon after, J.S. Place inherited the Nicomen Road House, which he quickly sold. He probably took some of the inventory to Dog Creek as the purchase agreement with Valenzuela included the packing of 7336 pounds of freight from Nicomen to Dog Creek. He also brought with him his expertise in running a roadhouse. Place's Hotel quickly became the most successful of the stores and hotels in Dog Creek in the 19th century.

J.S. met Miss Jane Ann Beaumont in Victoria on one of his trips for supplies. Jane was the governess to Governor Douglas's grandchildren. They married in Victoria on the 16th of July 1888.

The Places in Victoria.

The Places started their family on May 6th 1889 with a son, Frank.

Note of interest:

1) Samuel Leander Charles Brown was run over by a wagon on September 20th 1888. He died at Clinton, B.C.

2) The first school teacher at Empire Valley started to board at McEwen's February 26th 1888.

THE 1890'S

The other Place family children were born in the nineties .

    Joseph Smith Place Junior, April 14th 1890 in Dog Creek.

    Harry Beaumont Place, September 19th 1891 in Dog Creek.

    Annie Elizabeth Place, October 30th 1892 in Victoria.

    Charles Riley Place, March 25th 1894 in Victoria.

    William Place, October 26th 1896, Dog Creek.

Sadly, they lost two sons, Harry and William before their first birthday.

The Places, Annie, Jane and Charlie.

In the early nineties the new owners of Harper's property would make infrastructure changes that would be long lasting and would effect Dog Creek.

Thomas Dixon Galpin was the London source of funds for Thaddeus Harper's acquisition and development of his mining, ranching and milling ventures. When Galpin's offer to the courts for the purchase of the Gang Ranch was accepted, a limited company, Western Canadian Ranching Company was formed to manage the properties. It was registered in Victoria on March 26th 1891.

Mr. G.B. Martin was hired as manager. Mr. Cuyler Holland wrote to Galpin in August of 1891 with a detailed description of the different parcels that comprised the Gang at the time of purchase. He described the holdings in Dog Creek;

"The Dog Creek Ranch on the East side of the Frazer is at present useless to you. If we can sell at a reasonable figure we will do so; but it is overrun by the neighbors and we doubt if we could get our price".

In his evaluation of the Gang Ranch he wrote:

"…It is bounded by the Gaspard Creek, St. Mary's Creek (Churn Creek) & Frazer River…

We intend making this the headquarters, and shall apply to the Government for a road from Dog Creek to the top of the Gang benches. The probabilities are that we shall obtain this, and will then save some 32 miles of rough travelling, as at present the crossing is effected at Harper's Camp".(Lots 52,53 &54 at the mouth of the Chilcotin).

By 1890 there was a ferry running at the mouth of Churn Creek servicing the settlers of Empire Valley. The public accounts from June 1890 to July of 1891 shows a subsidy for the Canoe Creek ferry for $300.00 maintenance paid to C. Boyle.

Irrigation flume at Harper's Camp. C-188_.

In November of 1892, James Douglas Prentice manager , was urging the Company to apply for a charter for a ferry at the mouth of Churn Creek.

"It would be very awkward if an outsider were to secure this privilege and compel us to pay ferryage for crossing freight and on our own scow".

There seems to be a discrepancy on the above dates as there already was a ferry operating by November of 1892.

However without the road from the Ferry connected to Dog Creek, they would have to travel through Canoe Creek. This would have been an even longer trip than through Harper's Camp.

Approval was not given from the Government and the Gang built the road at their own expense. The B.C. Cattle Company complained to the Government that the road infringed on their land. The dispute was eventually settled with the Government compensating both parties.

Holland submitted a further detailed report in November with the intent to offer a prospectus to London investors and a view to the sale of the ranch. The Dog Creek property was not specifically mentioned.

**Churn Creek Ferry, April 14th 1904.
Photo by Frank Cyril Swannell.**

Note of interest:

Holland wrote to Galpin on November 11th 1890 about the formation of the B.C. Cattle Company;

"A local Company consisting of (Thomas) Ellis, (R.L.) Cawston, (R.P.)Rithet & (Captain John) Irving has just been formed with a capital of $ 300,000.00. They own property belonging to the first two (adjoining the Haynes Estate) and Van Volkenberg's properties (Canoe Creek etc.) on the highroad to Chilcotin some fourteen miles south of Dog Creek....".

The population of Dog Creek was beginning to diminish by the mid-nineties. With access to the West side of the Fraser via road and ferry, land and employment opened up for both whites and natives.

The Williams Directory of B.C. for Dog Creek listed only twenty five names. At least eight of these were situated in Empire Valley or on the Gang Ranch. Two of the residents listed in Williams Directory (1895) who were not living in Dog Creek were John Miller and his son John Junior. The Millers were listed as "ferrymen" for the Canoe Creek ferry and would have been living at the ferry crossing at Churn Creek.

John Mueller (Anglicized to Miller) was born in Kelso, Austria in 1831. Although Mueller was a tailor, gold was the attraction that brought him to Lillooet. Soon, however, reality set in and thus began his career as ferryman.

He was operating the ferry in Lillooet when he married a native, Julia Napoyet, of Fountain on the 22nd of February 1879. This job became redundant with the construction of a bridge crossing the Fraser.

**Canoe Creek Ferry (Churn Creek) c-1895.
John Miller, on right.**

The Williams Lake Tribune in the B.C. Centennial issue of 1958 wrote the following as part of the history of Dog Creek;

"An interesting character, Bill Wright, an American, who worked as a telegraph operator at Cache Creek came into the settlement. He married Placida, the daughter of Raphael Valenzuela and took up a large meadow between Grandview Ranch and Springhouse. He registered the letters U.S. as his brand and the property is still known as the U.S. Meadows. This action was resented by the Indians who predicted bad luck would come to any one who owned it. It may be regarded as pure coincidence that everyone but the present owner suffered heavy financial loss. Bill is the same chap as Bill Wright the ferryman in later days, a position he held until 1913 when he got his feet badly frozen and ultimately lost one leg. He recovered sufficiently to run the Soda Creek ferry for many years before passing on".

Ernest H. Thoresen, "The Fiddlin Swede" also knew Wright. In his memoirs he wrote the following anecdote;

"Another Character which I met in the Cariboo was a Frenchman who went by the name of Dynamite. I never knew his last name. A few years before I came to the country (1912), a man by the name of Bill Wright was in charge of the Churn Creek Ferry. Bill was a tough Missourian. It so happened that the Frenchman came down to the ferry on his saddle horse; Bill at this time was on the east side of the river with the ferry. The Frenchman hollered for the ferry to come across and pick him up. Well old Bill was busy on the east side so he did not come right away. The Frenchman was getting angrier and doing a lot of shouting. Finally the ferry came across and the Frenchman shook his fist in Bill's face and made a few insulting remarks; and you monkey with me you will be sorry for I am Dynamite when I get started. Bill said I am the man that set Dynamite off and with a swift uppercut knocked the Frenchman into the river. Bill seized a pike pole and pulled the near drowning man out of the river".

Bill Wright is in the group photograph of the St. Patrick's Day dance, 1911.

In 1895 there were three Chinese listed as traders. Yam Sing, Le Po George and Sing Lee. With Joseph Smith Place running the Dog Creek Hotel and Store this made four hotels and stores.

The Williams Lake Tribune published the following article by A.J. Drinkell on January 6th 1955;

Joy Sim, Dog Creek Merchant, Medicine Man and irrigator for J.S. Place.

"Chinese Move In

….From 1886 onward Mr. Place gradually bought out his Chinese competitors, a process that gained momentum as the gold pockets became harder to find. He took over the stock of the last store in 1909.

Of the Chinese who populated the valley at this time, several stand out in memory, such as George Li Po or "Chinese George". He was a very estimable man and highly regarded by all nationalities. Joy Sim or Ah Sim, as the Indians called him, was a merchant of Dog Creek, who had studied medicine in his homeland. He did an immense amount of good and affected some remarkable cures with his unguents and lotions. The latter were particularly potent, having a very firm alcoholic base. In this isolated area, where the nearest doctor was 100 miles away, and required a guarantee of $250.00 plus traveling expenses, in addition to his regular fees for professional services, and usually took so long to get there that by the time he arrived, the patient was either dead or out hunting again; the services of one so skilled as Joy Sim were totally beyond price".

"Charlie"
James Armes hired Charlie as cook for the Dog Creek house. He had been cooking at the snack bar of the Hudson Bay Co. in Vancouver. Unused to the cold weather of winter he returned to the coast the first fall.

Note of interest:

Thadeus Harper's obituary was printed in the "Prospector" Lillooet, on December 23rd 1898;

"Victoria, December 8th 1898 – Thadeus Harper, one time among the wealthiest citizens of the province, died today at the Jubilee here, after several months illness. With his brother Jerome he came to B.C. from California in 1858 and they amassed fortunes in trading beef and lumber with the miners of the Cariboo. When Jerome died, Thadeus became the sole manager of their extensive business and estate and all went well until an accidental kick from a horse effected his brain. Under changed conditions the business soon became involved in litigation which aided in virtual ruin of the estate. Mr. Harper had for a few years past resided in Victoria-He was a native of Virginia and 68 years of age".

Moses and Theresa Pigeon completed their family in the nineties. John Edgar (Eddie) was born June 9th 1894. The two girls of the family followed, Teresa, born February 13th 1896 and Agnes born February 10th 1898.

Eddie Pigeon.

The Pigeon Girls

Teresa,
Rose, (Claude's wife)
and
Agnes.
March 22nd 1913.

**Agnes Pigeon
14 years old**

The 1900s

Moses Pigeon passed away April 30th 1900. He was interred at the family graveyard on the Grandview Ranch. Responsibility of raising the surviving six children and running the ranch fell to the widow, Theresa. By all accounts she credited herself most successfully. As public education was unavailable in Dog Creek, Theresa sent the girls to New Westminster for their schooling.

Ray and Agnes Pigeon.

Rose and Claude Pigeon

Ray and Chrissie at the family cemetery, Grandview Ranch.

The Dog Creek Stage ran weekly from Clinton with mail, supplies and passengers. Photographer and surveyor, Frank Cyril Swannell, was a passenger in April 1904. He photographed the high water at Crazy Johnnies' on the 13th and the Churn Creek Ferry on the following day. The road conditions in the spring could be very unpredictable, to say the least.

High water on the Dog Creek Road.

The stage at Canoe Creek Canyon.

April 13th 1904 at Crazy Johnnies' Dog Creek Road.

Note of Interest:

1) Isadore Gaspard died April 21st 1898.

2) James Nathaniel Jerome Brown was the postmaster for Empire Valley from 1889 to 1892.

3) William Laing Meason Junior died November 11th 1902. He was staying at the Wycott's place in Empire Valley and had suffered from pneumonia for the previous two weeks. He was buried at the Meason Ranch at Little Dog Creek.

The Canadian Census was conducted again in the spring of 1901. It shows sixty two residents in the area bounded by the Meason ranch in the north , the Grandview ranch in the east, Nils Gustafson's River ranch in the west and Yam Sing's in the south. Forty were non Chinese and twenty two were Oriental.

Yam Sing was still operating his store where seventeen Chinese were listed as lodgers. He had been operating his enterprise for twenty five years when he sold his interest to Chew Gee on June 5th 1902 for $1.00.

Joseph S. Place's hotel and ranch were doing well. The census shows the six Place family members, a Chinese cook, Fouk Ko and four lodgers. The lodgers were in all probability employees of the ranch as the 1911 census lists three of them as servants or domestics.

One of these lodgers was Marc Pigeon, a cousin of Moses. Born in Quebec, he spent his life in Dog Creek. Simon Philipine, another lodger, was brother to Theresa Pigeon (nee Philipine). The third lodger that would put down roots in the Cariboo was Robert French, born June 16th 1879.

This was the decade that Joseph Smith Place expanded his holdings to include the last of his Chinese store competitors.

An article published in London in the 1912 book "British Columbia. It's History, People, Commerce, Industries and Resources" proclaimed the success and future possibilities of the Dog Creek Ranch. The land owners along the Fraser River were anticipating the construction of the new railroad on the west bank. Some of the ranches to be affected by this route were written about: Four Mile ranch, the Grange, Meason's Little Dog and the Dog Creek Ranch. Dog Creek was described as follows:

Back row-Joe Place Jr., Frank Place, Middle row- Mrs. J.E. Moore, Mr. J.E. Moore, Jane and Joe Place, Front row- Annie Place, Corpelis Moore. C-1911.

"Few ranches combine such a variety of classes of land as the Dog Creek Ranch, owned by Mr. J.S. Place. Lying between high mountains, it has a perpetual and abundant supply of water and irrigation offers no difficulty. The ranch consists of some 7,500 acres held under crown grant and a little over 2,000 acres held on lease, all of which, with the exception of a very small and unimportant part, is enclosed in a fence which is over 37 miles in length.... Since his purchase of the ranch in 1886, Mr. Place has been adding to it almost yearly, and the latest addition is Gaspard's farm, the crops of which, already luxuriant, can easily be doubled by the irrigation scheme which is being planned. The present ranch consists of the amalgamation of four ranches with other connecting lands....

Reference has already been made to the ease with which irrigation can be carried out. There is a ditch on the ranch which with its branches covers about 15 miles, and by its means over 600 acres have been placed under deep cultivation with hay, oats, wheat and barley and vegetables and small fruits, which do exceedingly well. The situation is considered quite suitable for peach growing, and the fact that an experiment with a few trees failed, is frankly admitted to be the result of lack of care and damage to the trees in transport to the ranch.

Stacking hay with the derrick at Dog Creek Ranch.

The stock held includes about 800 head of cattle, mostly shorthorns, and about 200 head of horses bred from Morgan and Percheron stock. Since 1909 there has been interbreeding with the Clydesdale strain, the chief stallion being Harlequin… There are about 30 pedigree bulls on the ranch, the chief of them being a Durham, for it is found that the judicious cross-breeding renders the cattle hardier and better able to stand the conditions of the ranch and of the long drive to the market at Ashcroft and the longer journey to Fort George, a place which is making demands which are materially benefiting the districts.

Harold Armes at the Gaspard farm with a fine example of a Dog Creek Horse.

The ranch buildings contain a store and stopping house, which is fully licensed, stabling for 25 horses, and also a small lumber and flour mill worked by an overshot water-wheel, generating about 16 horse power. Near the store is the old flour-mill building, now used as a shed, which is claimed to have been the first flour-mill on the mainland of the Province, having been built in 1866 (should be 1861). *For some years an extension of the residential buildings of the ranch has been under consideration, and the place favoured will greatly increase the accommodation of the stopping house to meet requirements, when the railway has been constructed on the farther bank of the Fraser River".*

The Dog Creek Sawmill, powered by the over-shot water-wheel. C-1917

William Laing Meason died at Little Dog on April 4th 1905. He had held his position as the Indian Agent for Williams Lake until he was seventy two years old. His obituary in the Ashcroft Journal concludes as follows:

"His later years were much saddened by the total loss of eyesight, but he ever retained a keen interest in the world's history and doings. A linguist of no mean ability, being well versed in French, Spanish and Latin languages. He is survived by three sons and three daughters and leaves a good estate, the result of his careful management, and the persevering industry of his stalwart sons".

When the boys finally disposed of the ranch Malcolm and Magnus moved to Hatzic Prairie to grow fruit and Gilbert moved to Hat Creek to ranch.

A large gathering on the porch of the Measons' Little Dog house, possibly for Christmas or a dance as the three at back right are holding musical instruments.

Left;
Large family gathering on the porch of the Little Dog House.
C-1919

Above; The Meason boys at Hatzic Prairie.

Above;
December 1909.

The book that published the previous article on the Dog Creek Ranch also covered the Meason Ranch at Little Dog Creek;

"....The whole ranch, which extends eight miles along the Fraser River spreading out to about four miles in width at distant points, is encircled with a fence some forty six miles in length including cross sections....

The land in the upper portions, however, has been disclosed to be particularly suitable for farming. Best done with alfalfa, oats, wheat and barley. The ranch possesses about three hundred acres of lowland on which fruit grows.

Area deemed suitable for dry farming is four thousand acres and the heavy rate for freight secures a local market for any produce at present. Advent of the railway on the other bank of the Fraser River will secure an outlet to other districts.

Cattle are mostly shorthorns which are favored by good winter pasturage, where dry feeding is seldom necessary.... As a result of careful game preservation for many years, the ranch affords fine sport with blue grouse, prairie chicken, geese and ducks and mule deer, while big horn sheep are to be found in neighboring mountains".

Above- The Meason Brother's Cattle at Little Dog. C-1912. At the time they were running seven hundred head.

Right- A display at Little Dog of the Measons' game trophies.

It seems that when the Chinese lost lives there was very little interest by the authorities to document or record the deaths, leaving the Chinese community to look after themselves. Consequently there is only one official death of a Chinese in Dog Creek recorded in the B.C. Archives in Victoria.

The exception to the rule was Dog Creek miner, Sat Chew. His death became official, as it was murder and an inquest was required.

An Alkali Lake native, Big Louie, was fishing on the Fraser at the mouth of Dog Creek the first week of September 1908 when he discovered the badly decomposed corpse of a man. Big Louie, suspecting the body to be Chinese, reported it to Ah Hing, the cook at the Dog Creek Hotel. He in turn told his friend Ah How who was working at the Meason Ranch at Little Dog Creek. The two Chinese visited the cabin and prepared the body for internment . They reported the death to How's employer, Malcolm Meason.

Meason made a trip to the cabin to confirm the tale. His inspection of the site brought him to the conclusion there had been foul play. An inquiry was soon set up. Jack McMillan, constable at Clinton, Joe Burr, Jack's boss from Ashcroft, Coroner Casper Phair, Dr. Cecil Boyd and Chief Joe Bacon of the Alkali Lake band as well as some local Chinese visited the scene of the crime.

It was established that the victim was in fact 65 year old Sat Chew. He had been a miner on the Fraser for the last seventeen years.

With the assistance of Joseph Smith Place, postmaster and storekeeper of the hotel, it was determined that Sat Chew had been in the store around the beginning of April. Chew had exchanged gold pannings for some grocery supplies. Of particular interest was the acquisition of three plugs of T&B Tobacco, and a five dollar bill. A clue, an old rusty revolver with a broken hammer, was discovered on the road to Alkali. Ah Hing identified it as belonging to Sat Chew. Constable Burr in his investigations became aware that there had recently been a large gathering of natives who had indulged in celebrations and gambling.

Two of the participants, Basil and Louie, were of particular interest. Basil had gambled and lost his 44 caliber rifle (the caliber that was used in the murder) and his friend Louie his three plugs of T&B tobacco. Arrests soon followed. January 1909, a preliminary hearing for the accused was held in Clinton. Confessions were obtained from both men. The only difference in their stories was who actually pulled the trigger. They each attributed this act to the other. The story took on a true wild west flavor as Louie cut bars and escaped from the Clinton jail, fast horse and all. He evaded capture for six months.

May 1910, both Basil and Louie were convicted. They were executed in Kamloops on July 20th 1910.

The Clinton Museum has this photo marked "Sat Chew".

Sat Chew was one of the last to pan for gold, it was beginning to become depleted along the Fraser and the Chinese moved on to other occupations. In 1908 Ah Hing was working for J.S. Place as the hotel cook, his Friend Ah How for Malcolm Meason at Little Dog and Ah Fook was an assistant packer for Jean Caux. Many Chinese hired out to the nearby ranches as cowhands and laborers.

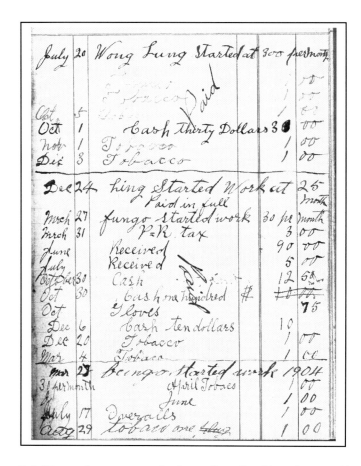

This is a page from McEwan's account ledger for the Empire Valley Ranch in 1902-3. It shows Wong Lung hiring on for $30.00 in July, Ling for $25.00 a month in December and Fungo for $30.00 in March. Wages would usually work out to $300 a year. Out of these wages they would have Provincial Revenue tax of $3.00 deducted.

Note of interest:

1) In the statement of accounts for the settlement of the wills of John and Anthony Bishop (Empire Valley) it shows three Chinese working for the ranch as laborers in 1924.

2) In the summer of 1889 the Gang Ranch had received approval for the construction of an irrigation ditch and flume. The Chinese and Indians were paid at the rate of $1.00 per day with board and the whites at $1.50. Labor apparently was readily available.

The Chinese went on strike in mid November due to an extreme cold snap. The manager advised the Western Canadian Ranching Co. :

"...Another ten days would have finished the ditch to below Bear Springs only leaving 7/8 of a mile to complete in the spring, The wages will amount to over $3000.00...".

**Lim Pow, Chinese cook with Geoff Place on Hotel porch.
C-1918.**

Some small Chinese medicine bottles excavated at the site of the Dog Creek Hotel. They date from around the first world war and could have possibly belonged to Lim Pow.

The above bottle (Carbolic Acid) also came from the same site. The clay pipes are embossed with the initials "ROAB". Ted Chevalier, a fellow explorer, solved the mystery for me. They stand for the Royal Order of Antediluvian Buffalo. Who had they belonged to, Oppenheimers, Gallagher, Valenzuela, Place or Drinkall? Whomever, they obviously were not in great demand and were discarded only to be recovered in the summer of 2006.

The 1910's

The Williams Lake Indian Agency enumerated the natives of the Dog creek reserve #1 on March 31st 1911. There were a total of fifty residents, some well known family names whose descendants are still in the area.

The Kalalest family, Betsy, Alex and their daughter Selina.
C-1909.

The Witte sisters in their book "Chilcotin: Preserving Pioneer Memories" wrote that Alex was the son of Joe Kala'llst a chief of a small band of Shushwaps that lived on the west side of the Fraser.

On the census, 28 year old Alex Kalalest was listed as the head of his household. His family consisted of wife Betsy, daughters Annie, Selearna and Metalan and son Peter.

Exactly when Alex moved his family from Dog Creek is unknown, but he settled on a quarter section (the north east corner) of district lot #3488, now part of the Gang Ranch. The title became official on the 15th of October 1954 when it was crown granted to Alex. The family raised cattle and horses and Alex would work away during the summer season.

Alex Kalalest and son Robbie showing one of their horses.

Hilary Place wrote about Alex;

"...he laughed the loudest and told the funniest stories out of all of them... During the summer Alex stayed with his wife and family in a camp of tents set up by the ditch behind the blacksmith shop where he worked at several different tasks. Besides blacksmithing, he also made rawhide ropes, fixed saddles, and taught some of the younger men how to do things with horses and cattle.

Alex's wife didn't speak any English, yet you felt she understood everything because she was always smiling and taking part in the goings-on. Their daughter Selena was also a very happy girl, despite the fact she was badly crippled by a congenital birth defect in her pelvis....

When fall came, Alex and his family packed their things and returned to their own place between the Gang and Big Creek...."

Alex died at Dog Creek March 14th 1964 aged 79.

The Dog Creek Reserve #1, 1914.

The Williams Lake Tribune published an article in 1992 titled "Natives first Residents". The following is an excerpt from the "Nostalgia" series;

".... The two reserves at Dog Creek are known as Reserve #1 and a few miles up the valley Reserve #2.... Another small reserve up on the mountain six miles away, four abandoned log homes still mark the site of their old village called Tsek-7....

Disaster struck in the 1880s when smallpox almost wiped out the tribe; later flu epidemic and other illnesses would take their toll. Even in the 1950s there were only four families living on the reserve..."

In 1911 the census shows the head of the Robin household was known only as "Robin". He was living with his two sons, Felix 16 and Moses 14. Williams Lake Tribune wrote in 1958; "*...Robins a member of the Alkali Indian Band...Spent much of his time in Dog Creek. For many seasons he accompanied Cataline's pack train to the northern posts of the Hudson's Bay Co. He was a kindly, gentle soul and a keen lover of animals. He also had a penchant for Hudson Bay rum which he could quaff with great circumspection. He passed away at Alkali Lake almost at the century mark".*

This photo was marked "Old Robin, almost 100years old".

St. Patrick's Day Dance, March 17th 1911 at the Dog Creek House.

The following description of the above photograph was published in the Williams Lake Tribune in the 1958 Centennial issue.

"The above photograph was taken following a dance given at Dog Creek in 1911. That young fellow standing at the extreme left is Claude Pigeon, who at that time, was the mainstay of the family ranch. Until retiring recently he was for many years the local agent for Shell Oil Co. The dignified gentleman standing near the center is John E. Moore who had large holdings at both Alkali Lake and Onward Ranch. He is flanked by daughters Marie on the left and Dilly on the right. The lady standing at the far right is Mrs. Alex Meiss (nee-Matilda Gaspard). Second from the left seated is T.S. Patton who also may still be found around town. Anyone requiring the services of a tip-top caller for square-dances should lure Tom into the dance hall. Next to him is Bill Wright who for many years operated the government ferry near the mouth of Churn Creek. A book could be written about Bill. A telegrapher by profession he manipulated the keys in the Cache Creek office in the really early days. He married Placida, daughter of Rafael Valenzuela and took up ranching at what became known as U.S. Meadows the U.S. being

his registered brand. He gave up farming to operate the ferry. His last assignment was to operate the ferry at Soda Creek. Protruding from behind the arm of host J.S. Place may be seen the face of Pablo Tresierra, of Mexican origin; a first rate sawyer and woodsman. Next is Stefano Mondada; at the extreme right is Antonio Boitanio who ranched for many years at Springhouse but is now retired. That beaming face pressed forward at the very back of the picture belonged to Joe Smith who was the foreman at the Wynn-Johnson ranch at Alkali Lake in those days".

In the latter part of November, 1913, Ernie Thoresen, a recent arrival at Big Bar Mountain, was working near Clinton, building the grade for the future Pacific Great Eastern Railway. He received a letter from J.S. Place at Dog Creek stating that they were putting on a New Years Eve dance and wanted Ernie to furnish the music. He describes it in his "Memories of the Cariboo" as follows:

**Ernest H. Thoresen
"The Fiddlin Swede"**

"Well I quit my job with the railroad, saddled my horse and took off for Dog Creek. I got there the day before New Years Eve. People came for many miles around for the festival which lasted two nights I was quite tired as they never let up dancing till daylight".

Ernie stayed in the Cariboo for many years. He became locally famous for his music and became known as "The Fiddlin Swede".

A.J. Drinkell, in his unpublished biography of Ada Place described these occasions as follows;

"Neighbors were a considerable distance apart, twelve miles in any direction. Occasionally a dance brought them together but the unpredictable nature of ranch operations prevented acceptance of invitations to visit on slated dates or times.

It had been customary during the Christmas holidays to load the ladies and children in sleighs together with a demi-john or two of rum. With the men folk mounted on their saddle horse they would converge on a neighboring ranch. Dancing would occupy the entire night. The next day some of the men returned to their respective spreads to feed the livestock and do other necessary chores. The remainder would escort the ladies and children to the next ranch.

This procedure was followed during the whole of the week so that by the New Year's Eve the whole kit and caboodle would be foregathered at one place for a fitting climax to the festive season".

Note of interest;

1) The eight acre parcel of land that the original grist mill sat on in the 60s was pre-empted by Frank Place on May 17th 1911. Lot #2288 also encompassed the hillside south of the creek known as Rabbit Park.

2) Eleanor Laing Meason married John McLuckie December 15th 1913.

3) Annie Meason married James Michael Scanlon January 16th 1918 at Springhouse.

Jean Caux, better known as "Cataline" has had much written about his exploits, some true . Ernie Thoresen arrived in the spring of 1912 at the Dog Creek Hotel, meeting Cataline and joining his crew on a pack trip north. At this time Cataline was nearing the end of his packing career and had wintered his stock of 83 horses and mules in Dog Creek. His crew for this trip was Serape Leon, a Mexican, Pablo Tresierra, Dave McDaniels, William Vaughn and two natives from Highbar, Skokum Joe and Antwyne , last but not least a strapping Irishman, Rufe Evans.

Cataline had a contract with the B.C. Government, at that time, to pack supplies for the telegraph stations between Hazelton and Dawson, Yukon Territory.

**Cataline loading mule pack train in Ashcroft.
L-R, Alphonse Loring, Peter Hymaben (Kispiox Indian-brother in law to B.C. outlaw Simon Peter Gunanoot), Cataline, Dave Wiggins, Gavin Hamilton (back to camera).
Not shown is Chinese, Ah Fook, Cataline's assistant.**

The following is a first hand account of this trip by Ernest Thoresen.

"At that time he was 83 years of age, tall, powerfully built at least 200 pounds in weight. He wore his hair long, down to his shoulders. His speech was broken. He talked slow but had a powerful voice. He was born in 1829 near the border of Spain and France. He left Barcelona Spain on a sailing ship the year of 1847 bound for Cuba, eventually arriving in the United States that same year. The following spring making his way across the plains to Oregon with an immigrant train he acquired a plot of land in the middle of Portland Oregon. Leaving Portland in 1855 he arrived in Yale, British Columbia. He made his first pack train trip in 1855 to the remote interior of B.C.

He and Pablo when together always spoke Spanish. But he could also speak the Indian language as I later found out."

Jean Caux, in his retirement years in Hazelton, B.C.

"One trait I observed of Cataline, when at the bar having a drink, no mixed drinks, all drinks neat. He would always leave a little whiskey in the glass and then empty the glass on his head and rub it in his scalp. ….He did not drink liquor in camp or on the trail. Another thing I noticed when he bought a pair of cowboy boots in Dog Creek, he put them on and went out and stood in the horse trough for quite some time".

Ernie described the trip north and the many stops visiting the ranches and people that are now part of the early Cariboo history. He wrote;

"We traveled steadily up the Cariboo Road. Every night sitting around the campfire. I was an attentive listener and enjoyed every minute. One evening Cataline was taking a wash in a nearby creek and I noticed a large scar on his left forearm. I asked him what had happened to his arm. He laughed and said that happened many years ago. So at the campfire that evening he told the following story. "I was packing for some miners out of Yale, British Columbia, the year was 1857. The trip lasted 27 days into south eastern B.C. I returned to Yale and put my mules in a corral near the river. That evening before going to bed I decided to go down and see if my mules were well supplied with hay. On my way back two men jumped me armed with knives. I threw up my left arm to ward off the knife at the same time I hit him in the jaw with my right fist and with a swift kick caught the other robber in the stomach. I grabbed the two of them by the collar and dragged them up to the jail. The next morning these two men were aboard a steamer heading down river. They were in bad shape. Ned McGowan, bad man from California, ruled the roost of Yale in the early days and these two robbers were no doubt members of his gang. Yale was tough and there were killings most every day. Cataline laughed and said " I don't think those hombres enjoyed a meal for quite some time".

The pack train was north of Hazelton when Ernie was told that from here on only ½ the horses and mules would be required for the packing. Antwyne, Skokum Joe and Ernie were elected to return with the excess animals. He writes;

Next morning we had breakfast together for the last time. Cataline said as he shook my hand, "Don't go around kissing the wolf " and with a laugh said " I may see you next spring". Cataline was a rough tough man but he was an honest man and never went back on his word. Well we saddled up and with 39 head of horses we took off down the trail. That was the last time I saw Cataline. He made one more trip in 1913, the last. He died in Hazelton in 1922 and is buried there".

More examples of Jean Caux's legend building exploits were published in the Lillooet, Bridge River newspaper on September 24th 1936. You be the judge of their credibility.

The credits following the article were;

"This editorial on Game was dictated by Peter Colin, (Pierre Collin's son) a native son of Cariboo, whose father is French. Witnessing it was Alonzo Tresierra, native son of Yale, B.C., whose father was Spanish and a partner of Cataline. Mr. Colin's father, Alonzo's father and S.C. Leander Brown were packers for Onderdonk on C.P.R. construction. The facts were told in the bunkhouse at the O.K. Ranch, Big Bar as can be testified to by Bill Bunnage, ranch boss for Harry Marriott".

The title on the article was;

"Sportsmanship in The Game Country"

"Jean Cataline, the mighty packer, who used to take his train from Ashcroft as far north as Telegraph Creek, over a trail which may one day be the route of the Alaska Highway, had a code of honor which he observed to the letter.

Jean Cataline would never take more than two glasses of rum-one to drink and the other to rub into his luxuriant head of hair.

He was chivalrous towards the Indians, more particularly towards the young Indian women.

He would never engage in a brawl; but would fight if a man called him a certain name without smiling.

Jean Cataline kept no books, but always remembered every item of the business which passed through his hands and was prompt to pay if he had the money.

Now Cataline traveled from his headquarters at Dog Creek to Hazelton, and beyond through a game paradise. Often, the grouse ran before the train as the bell mare rounded a turn. Grouse and pheasants were plentiful enough in those days.

Cataline would never kill save for food. Once his cargodore discharged a shotgun into a covey of grouse killing six, and Cataline almost fired the man on the spot. Woe to the servilano in the train who killed more game than the needs of the moment called for.

Cataline always carried small stones in his saddlebag. When he wanted a bird, he gave the bird a chance. If Cataline with his left arm could not hurl a stone straight enough to kill a pheasant at twenty yards, he would go hungry.

Cataline never loaded down his kitchen horse with meat which later would be cast out to spoil.

Jean Cataline, mighty packer of the early days of Cariboo was a sportsman. He set an example which hunters of this day and generation going into Bridge River, Lillooet, Clinton, Quesnel, Prince George or Fort St. John could well follow".

Jean Caux's blacksmith on the trip of 1912 was Serape Leon. Serape was born at Douglas Lake. The B.C. Archives lists his mother as Louise, his father as Blas Leon and his birth date as 1867. Blas Leon was a packer and quite conceivably was the "Leon" that Leon's Station was named after. Leon's station was a road house situated on the Fraser River at Highbar. Serape was only ten years old when in 1877, his father was killed by a tree falling on him. Serape grew up living in various households in the area. He married a local girl, Elizabeth Hinck, on the 30th of July 1903. The wedding took place at the Indian Church at Highbar. He was 34 years old and she was 15.

In 1913 Ernie Thoresen was living at Big Bar when he visited Serape, who was living just north of the Big Bar ferry on the west side of the Fraser. This would probably have been at French Bar, across the river from the Hinck's homestead. Serape worked at the Gang as blacksmith and shows up on the 1911 census as having worked on a road crew. He died at Ashcroft July 7th 1926 aged 56.

Serape Leon's wife Elizabeth. (Nee- Hinck)

The first Place child to leave the fold was Annie. She was 18 when she married Francis Douglan Lindsay in Ashcroft on August 26th 1911.

Annie Elizabeth Place.

Like the Pigeon girls, Annie was educated at a Vancouver Finishing school. Her nephew, Hilary Place, described her as being beautiful, having the

"….social graces of a debutante, but she could also ride a rough horse and cowboy with the best of the men".

Lindsay was with the bank in Ashcroft but soon after marriage he formed an early taxi and freight company that was to compete with the B.X. Company. It was offering passage from Ashcroft to points north, the northern terminus was Soda Creek.

The company consisted of three early automobiles that in good times were never too reliable. They dated from 1908 to 1910. In addition to the lack of services available the road conditions were only receptive to auto traffic in the summer.

An example of the road conditions that could be encountered on the Cariboo Road. The leaning gentleman and woman on the right are Charles and Mary Doering, owners of the Hat Creek House on a road trip in 1912.

Annie Place at Dog Creek.

The inevitable occurred and the company was soon experiencing financial difficulties. Annie appealed to her father Joseph. J.S. responded, bailing them out and assuming title of the three automobile assets that were then transported to Dog Creek. Place put the autos to private use and closed the transportation business.

Although they had two children, Douglas and Doris, they separated and divorced.

Annie married a second time, Alfred Joseph Drinkell, a recent arrival in Dog Creek. This marriage was short lived but made A.J. a relative to the Place family by marriage.

Alfred Joseph Drinkell, known as "Drink" arrived in Dog Creek in 1913. He arrived from Jesmond where he had been employed by Harry Coldwell at the Mountain House. (The children of Dog Creek called him "Dink").

A.J. was born in Grimsby in Lincolnshire county in 1888 and arrived in British Columbia from England in 1911. J.S. Place hired Drinkell in 1913 as storekeeper which also involved acting as postmaster, bartender and private secretary.

A.J. Drinkell was the official postmaster in Dog Creek from July 1924 until February of 1962. He replaced J.S. Place who had held the position from 1886 until his death in 1924.

Drinkell described a disagreement with Mrs. Jane Place during one of J.S.'s absences;

"I foolishly allowed myself to become involved in an argument with Mrs. Place one afternoon during her husband's absence.

Some of the bar patrons got a little boisterous but not at all quarrelsome. One chappie named Dan Smith, was singing with great gusto, "Throw out the life line, someone is sinking today".

Whether Mrs. Place thought this was sacrilegious or misjudged the nature of the crowd I really don't know but she ordered me to close down the bar.

I ventured the opinion I could not legally do so and in the ensuing argument I expressed myself rather impolitely. A further exchange of "compliments" took place when her sons came in from work.

Upon Mr. Place's return some days later I resigned my position, and was in bad odor for some time".

Drinkell went north briefly, only as far as Alkali Lake. Mr. Wynn-Johnson who owned the Alkali Lake store, was injured when he was thrown from his cart. Drinkell managed the store until his recovery was complete. When he left Alkali, headed for the Mountain House , he stopped at The Dog Creek Store and Post Office and stayed. He was to be an integral part of the

history of Dog Creek for next 40 years .

In 1912 the store and post office were moved out of the hotel into a new commodious building across the street. The new barn was also built at this time, replacing several smaller buildings.

The Dog Creek store "Ranchers Retail" or "The Dog Creek Trading Company" when Drinkell ran it. C-1947.

A scarce example of an early postcard Souvenir of Dog Creek. C-1910.

A.J.'s profession was accountant. He described himself: *"My chief interests were sports, politics and the study of human nature. Classified by some as a dreamer and by others as "that Englishman".*

To the above we can also add historian. He wrote articles for the Williams Lake Tribune on local history and spoke occasionally to the Williams Lake Historical Society.

Ada Halstead Netherwood was from Hudderfield, Yorkshire, England and arrived in dog Creek April 1914. She very soon became the dominant personality in Dog Creek.

She was 28 years old and had been convalescing for some time from a protracted illness, the result of the termination of her engagement to a young man, a Fellow of Cambridge University. Apparently she had what they would refer to as a delicate nature.

Before her arrival in British Columbia her father had taken her to Egypt and France on a trip to assist in her recovery. Slowly recovering she accepted an invitation to visit New York from a family friend Mrs. Robertshaw. From

**Ada, Joe and Jane.
April 1914.**

New York she traveled to Nanaimo where family friends, the Blenkhorns, were operating a chicken farm. It was here that Jane Place became aware that the daughter of a schoolmate was in British Columbia and she immediately wrote and extended an invitation to Ada to visit the Place Ranch at Dog Creek.

Ada accepted and stayed. She married Charles Riley Place the youngest son of Jane and Joseph on August 8th 1914 at Ashcroft.

Wedding day, August 8th 1914, Ashcroft.

Ada and Charlie's first son, Charles Geoffrey was born in Ashcroft on May 18th 1915.

Ada's parents had given the newlyweds a paid trip back to England for a wedding present. Unfortunately the World War precluded any unnecessary travel and it had to be postponed until after the armistice.

Joseph Smith Place Junior, after Charlie, was the next to get married. He married Miss Violet Ella Lyne from Ashcroft on November 16th 1915.

Violet's parents, William and Angelique Lyne, were the proprietors of the Ashcroft Hotel.

**Joe and Violet Place.
November 16th 1915.**

**William and Angelique Lyne.
(nee-Dussault).In 1914 they were running a Hotel
at Nine Mile Creek, c/o Soda Creek P.O.**

Joe and Violet started their married life in Dog Creek in temporary quarters, the "White House", an empty building on Yam Sing's lot. Their first child Jean was born while they were living there. Joe was working as foreman for his father on the family ranch.

They pre-empted lot #4389 on the south side of the creek just west of the wagon road leading to the Gang Ranch. Construction was started on permanent housing that was to become known as the View Ranch.

Joe and Violet had four more children while living here, Harold, Millie, Kathleen and Joyce. Joe continued to live there until 1953. His daughter Millie and husband had just moved out to the Canim Lake area. The last winter that Joe put in at the View Ranch he burned the logs and lumber from the chicken coop, garage and barns for firewood.

Above- The View Ranch house.

Right- Four Place girls, Millie, Paddy, Jean and Evelyn.

Jean with her horse At the View Ranch.

Harold Place.

Kathleen Ella Place.

Joseph Smith Place Jr. with his daughter, Kathleen Ella and his sister in law, Clara Johnson (nee-Lyne)

The war years were not kind to the Place family. Jane was afflicted with cancer and had an unsuccessful operation in Victoria. She lingered for some time before passing away April 19th 1918.

The settlement of the son-in-law's debts would eventually lead to an insurmountable cash flow problem. The ability to operate the ranch profitably was restricted as J.S. had sold some of the cattle to cover the debts and it was the herd that generated the profit.

During this decade J.S. had expanded his holdings to include Pierre Collin's pre-emption as well as the Meason brothers' ranch that the brothers had increased to 13,000 acres. These additions would also increase his inability to recover.

The obligations that J.S. took on with the Lindsay bankruptcy were not popular with the rest of the family. The three sons, at this time, acquired lots of their own. Frank already had the 160 acres of lot 2288, Young Joe took up lot 4389 and Charlie acquired what was referred to as D-4, west of the Gaspard Ranch. D-4 was Charlie's registered brand. Charlie and Ada's first home was the small cabin situated on the original eight acres that were settled by Brown and the original grist mill.

The log portion of "Little Casey," what was to become "Casa Grande".

A.J. Drinkell wrote of the foreclosure;

"In due course the people holding the mortgage on the Dog Creek Ranch decided to foreclose causing the other creditors to exercise their powers under the "Deed of Trust." The author (A.J. Drinkell) was instrumental in effecting a settlement under which the liquid assets were brought in and the land leased under a long term agreement whereby the estate was divided into a series of compact units and a valuation placed upon each unit. The three sons were accorded the opportunity to acquire one unit each and Charlie chose a unit known as Big Lake Meadows situated near Gustafson Lake at the headwaters of Dog creek and some thirty miles east of D-4."

Frank was the last of the children to marry. He married, Francis Opal Lyne, a sister of young Joe's wife, Violet. They were married in Vancouver on January 17th 1917.

Frank's unit of choice was the River Ranch. He worked and lived on this lot until his death on January 25th 1940.

In the spring of 1919,the war now over, Ada and Charlie took the trip to England, a wedding gift from her parents. Charlie stayed for the summer and returned in the fall to look after their place, putting the finishing touch on the house he built on D-4.

Hilary was born in March 1920 but as both Geoff and Ada were ill the return to Dog Creek was not until October 1920.

In the breaking up of the Place holdings into small parcels, A.J. Drinkell assumed the portion that included "Casey" ,the sawmill and store. He and Charlie formed a partnership that was to be long lasting.

Note of Interest;

1) With the foreclosure of the mortgage on the ranch, just after the war, the Meason Ranch had been acquired by Mr. William Holden at a tax sale.

2) By the time Ada arrived back in Dog Creek in the fall of 1920, Joseph Place Senior had left for Victoria where he married Miss Ethel Ross.

THE 1920'S

James Langman Armes and his wife Maude Evelyn at Dog Creek.

James Langman Armes, an entrepreneur, speculator and an overall general promoter married Maude Evelyn Hobinstock on the 23rd March 1920.

This was his second marriage. James had four children from his first marriage, Frank, Kathleen (Kitty), Harold and Harvey.

James was from the west country market town of Tavistock on the Tavey river in Devon England. One of his early enterprises was a company that provided bottled mineral water.

The Armes family came into possession of the Meason Ranch through a negotiated agreement with William Holden, owner at the time. Not long after this transaction James became aware that the Dog Creek Hotel and ranch was in foreclosure. By taking over an assumption of the mortgage, he was able to add the portions of the ranch not taken up by the Place boys and Drinkell to his growing holdings in Dog Creek.

Frank Armes, 1913.

Frank was the son that was to have the longest association with the Dog Creek area. He had been attending college in Vancouver with the intent of becoming a purser on a steamship line when at 16, his dad took him out of college. He bought him a sheepskin coat and other suitable Cariboo clothes and sent him off to Dog Creek. Doreen Armes, Frank's future wife, writes of his arrival in her "Memory Journal";

".... arriving in Clinton on New Years Day 1924 to be met by A.J. Drinkell, postmaster and storekeeper in Dog Creek. His brother Harold was the ostensible manager of the ranch but he had no interest in agricultural pursuits preferring to take up his duties from an armchair in the Dog Creek House with Kitty (and children) his sister as cook and housekeeper and keeping informed re cattle and range through questioning Frank and Dave Thompson, cowboy, in the evenings. It was fortunate that Frank's camp companion was George Wright a seasoned cowman and capable cowboy".

The Thompson family, Dave, Grace, Mrs. Thompson, Flo and Bob. Posing against the Armes' Graham-Paige at the Dog Creek House. C-1927.

George Wright had a small cabin beside Vert Lake on Dog Creek Mountain. Brother in law to A. J. Drinkell, he was born in England and arrived in Dog Creek in 1910. George died on December 19th 1925 in Dog Creek, a result of heart failure, at only 50 years of age. He had suffered for some time from an enlarged heart. A. J. Drinkell looked after the funeral arrangements and he was buried in Rabbit Park on lot 2288.

A survey of his cabin site in the summer of 2006 unearthed a few unbroken bottles. It was obvious that George had a penchant for Gin, as many of the empty bottles were discovered, mostly broken.

**The author at the site of George Wright's cabin, with a very nice Chinese Ginger pot and a broken stoneware Dutch Gin.
May 2006.**

Note of interest:

Marc Pigeon married Placida Florence Valenzuela at the Grandview Ranch on April 2nd 1927. He was 54, she was 63.

Not wanting to raise the children without a proper education, Ada wanted to have a school started in Dog creek. Drinkell, who owned and was living in the small cabin that Ada was later to christen "Casa Grande" offered the use of the premises. As there was a requirement for eight children to live within three miles of the school in order to comply with the Public School Act, Ada and Charlie moved from D-4 in order to qualify.

The Department of Education approved the school and awarded a grant of $150.00 towards the cost of construction. Doors, windows and shingles were purchased with the grant.

The original Dog Creek school as it looked in 1946.

Drinkell described the effort:

"Sufficient logs were at the mill to provide the thirteen thousand board feet of lumber required for the edifice.. These and the use of the sawmill and planer constituted my contribution to the project....

Some of the parents leveled the building site and laid the foundation logs. Charles and I did the rest. It was December and bitterly cold but the school had to be open immediately after the New Year. We shingled the roof in sub-zero weather. Wind made it impossible to do other than lay the shingles one by one. Nails could not be held in the mouth as they would stick to the lips. We overcame the difficulty by one holding the shingle in place while the other nailed it down; taking turns with the hammer.

The school was completed in time. It was a two room structure having two concrete chimneys. One room was equipped with clothes racks, table forms, crockery and a small cook stove so that lunches could be warmed in cold weather and garments dried....

Ed Hillman painted it in the spring. A teacher was appointed by the Department and her salary paid entirely by them."

Miss Pansy Price, first teacher at Dog Creek. C-1927.

The school was opened in January 1926. The first teacher was Miss Pansy Price. Miss Price, from Victoria, was a recent graduate of Normal School and Dog Creek was her first school. She returned for the 1926-1927 school year.

At a time when most of the one-room schools were constructed of logs, Alex Lord described the Dog Creek School as *"...an unusually attractive building"*, in his "Recollections Of a Rural School Inspector". Lord was an inspector of schools for the district.

The final construction of the school was the flooring. Machined flooring was not available at the time of construction. The laying of the floor was done by the volunteer efforts of a B.C. Telephone crew stationed in Dog Creek.

A.J. Drinkell wrote of the phone system;

"A telephone line previously built from Clinton to the Gang Ranch was extended to Williams Lake via Dog Creek and Alkali Lake. This was a single wire installation having a buzzer signaling system. A hornlike gadget dubbed "a howler" emitted the signals.

Its main purpose was to lighten the load on the main telegraph line running north from Ashcroft. Telegrams could be transmitted over it even when in conversational use.

The howler also doubled as a loud speaker as every sound along the line was audible through it giving it the semblance of a public address system. Consequently, it was not unusual for some of the folks when about to impart a choice piece of gossip, to preface their remarks with the forthright statement "I hear by the phone".

The telephone crew that laid the finished flooring on the new school. C-1927.

Nevertheless it was a great boon to us who had been so long with no other means of communication than the uncertain mail service and the regional "moccasin telegraph".

Most evenings found the men at Casa Grande where they were warmly welcomed and served light refreshment before retiring to camp. As a token of appreciation the crew laid a finishing floor in the school for which there had not been material or opportunity previously".

Drinkell wrote of the initial reception and acceptance of the telephone by the natives:

"She (Ada Place) *was frequently called upon to make telephone connections between local Indians and their distant friends, also to act as intermediary.*

Eventually, however they overcame their reluctance to become familiar with this new talking machine and did their own talking once the connection was established.

Making a connection was not a simple matter in some instances; first of all a call would be made to a telephone subscriber nearest the reservation required, asking that a messenger be sent to get the wanted party to the telephone. This might take a couple of days to accomplish. The next step was to arrange a time for both parties to be on hand so the connection could be completed".

Note of interest:

1) Joseph Smith Place died in Victoria on May 2nd 1924.
2) Theresa Meason (nee Tuccatone) died at Upper Chimney Creek in the winter of 1929. *"Her daughters, Theresa, Celestine and Annie held a prayer vigil for her all night saying the rosary and keeping the candles burning-The Native way".*

1929 and another brand new teacher for the Dog Creek school, Doreen Pollitt. Miss Pollitt started her education in Edmonton and moved to Vancouver in 1925 where she completed grade thirteen and normal school. This gave her the opportunity for a first class teaching certificate.

Unable to get a job in the city or even nearby, she looked to the interior. Only two positions were available, Queen Charlottes and Dog Creek.

Doreen Pollitt, the new teacher for 1929. Doreen became a long time resident of Dog Creek and the Cariboo.

On her arrival in Dog Creek, Miss Pollitt made arrangements to be boarded at the Hotel. Her room was what used to be the music room and the room and board cost was $30.00 per month. In the depression, money received for the board of the teacher was cash to be coveted.

The hotel at the time of her arrival was operated by the Armes family. Kathleen (Kitty) was the housekeeper and her brother Harold was the manager of the ranch. Kitty had her three children, Eric and Betty Earle and the baby Gladys. The hotel had more than adequate space as it contained twenty two rooms.

These two cowboys, Hilary and Geoff were living at Casa Grande when this picture was taken. C-1929. The lady is unidentified, The building in the background was the blacksmith shop for the ranch.

Gladys Barnwell, Kitty's daughter at the Dog Creek house.

Hilary Place, Pete, Bubbles, Geoffrey and Harold Place.
"Bubbles" was Nora (Toby) Clyne's sister.
Below-Jean and Millie Place with a 1929 Chev & two puppies.

The following page clockwise from the top,
Two visiting nieces of Nora (Toby) Clyne and Eric Oliver with the Armes' Graham-Paige.
Hilary and Geoff on Hilary's 12th birthday.
Dog Creek Hotel guests from the 20's.
"Bubbles", Toby's sister.

THE 1930'S

1930 was the year that James L. Armes saw, because of the depression, that there was no future in cattle or the hotel business in Dog Creek.

The original mortgage holder once again exercised his rights and the Dog Creek Hotel was offered to the partnership of Charlie Place and A.J. Drinkell. The old stopping house and fifteen hundred acres were purchased at a very attractive price and terms.

Once again the Place family had an interest in the Dog Creek Hotel.

Joseph Smith Place Junior at the Dog Creek Hotel, again in the Place family and the precarious depression ahead.

Drinkell wrote a brief history of the additions and changes that were made over the years to the Hotel;

"These included a two story ELL, built upon the occasion of his marriage to Jane Anne Beaumont, to provide a sitting room and two bedrooms for their private use; also included were a kitchen and laundry. Later came another lean-to to house a bar, bar-parlour and washroom.

In 1912, partly in order to meet the requirements of a newly enacted Liquor Act, but mainly in preparation for an anticipated growth of the settlement due to the fact the original plans called for the Pacific Great Eastern Railroad to follow the Fraser River after leaving Lillooet, a new two storey store was erected across the street from the hotel with the upper storey laid out for bedrooms, etc.

The space occupied by the old store was converted into a sitting room and two bedrooms. The old kitchen was also made into a bedroom. A new kitchen with three bedrooms overhead was also added at that time along with a concrete structure to serve as a milk house and dairy.

Like most of the old time stopping houses it was decorated and furnished more from the viewpoint of utilitarianism than personal comfort;...."

It was this that Charlie, Ada, Geoff, Hilary and Drinkell moved into in 1930. Accommodations this large required hired help. Drinkell wrote of one of the earliest local native girls hired as housekeeper;

"Mrs. Charlie decided to try out an Indian girl, named Elsie Mashue, who had just completed her studies at the district Indian Residential School.

Elsie proved quick to learn, was very well mannered and as neat and clean as a new pin. She spoke good English. She and her mistress soon learned to understand each other and got along very well.

Elsie remained until her marriage some two years in all and was missed by every member of the household".

Drinkell wrote of the difference in priorities between the two cultures., the need for the natives to leave for berry season, fishing or the funeral of a forty second cousin. Understandable, as the food contributed heavily to their winter supplies: *"Notwithstanding these handicaps the house was kept spotlessly clean, all meals served on time and afternoon tea sipped with customary formality"*.

Conditions on the reserve have improved over the years. Doreen Armes wrote of her observed changes from the thirties to the present; *"Thank goodness the housing on the reserves today is of an acceptable standard, at least it appears so from the outside. When I recall Dog Creek Reserve all I see are low log buildings with small paned windows and few of those. An average height Caucasian male would have to duck to get in the door, many didn't have wooden floors but the dirt was hard packed. Furniture seemed to consist of blocks of wood to sit on, a table to hold everything and anything and a couple of orange crates on the wall to hold a few utensils. Blankets stacked against a wall would suggest sleeping arrangements...."*.

Elsie, her mother Eliza Mashue, brother Basil and unidentified at Eliza's cabin on the Dog Creek reserve. C-1933.

A very long lasting relationship between Elsie and Walter Gaspard was entered into with their wedding in 1935. They remained married for 59 years.

Walter Gaspard began cowboying for the Gang Ranch in 1925, when he was fourteen. He soon became an excellent cattleman and horse trainer, breaking and training rough stock. All together, Walter and Elsie had ten children, Burt, Violet, Rose, Marvin, William, Frank, Lillian, Gordon, Doreen and Barbara.

The family stayed in Dog Creek until 1948 when Walter got employment in William's Lake working for the railroad.

Rose, Marvin and Violet Gaspard.

Walter, his son Burt and Willy Billy at the Gang Ranch.

Grandson, Gordon Gaspard wrote of Walter;

"In the 1970's, his family grown up and moved on, Walter turned again to the cowboy life, the life he loved. He ultimately worked for the Gang Ranch on and off for over fifty years. Walter also worked on many other ranches in the interior, The Douglas Lake, and the Koster Ranch among them".

Walter passed away on March 20th 1995 aged 83.

Elsie Euphtasia passed away December 27th 2001, aged 87.

Charlie Brown moved his family west to the Empire Valley after the dissolution of the grist mill partnership with Isadore Gaspard. Using the original set of burrs, Charlie set up another mill, the "Excelsior Mills". His first son James Nathaniel Jerome Brown was, in his own words "...*born in the middle of the Lillooet Trail with only the pine trees above me. My parents were driving home from the fourth of July Celebration at Barkerville. Barkerville was mostly American in the days of the gold rush, so the fourth of July was our big holiday*".

James Nathaniel Jerome Brown.

Jim Brown gave an interview to the Vancouver Sun in July 1938 on the celebration of his 75th birthday.

"Born on the Lillooet Trail"

"Mr. Brown has spent three-quarters of a century in British Columbia as prospector, cowboy, newspaper editor and poet.

He attributes his good health to the fact that he has never touched liquor.
"It was a hard thing to stay an abstainer back in those days. Those old timers were about the hardest drinking lot that ever lived. I used to treat them all once in a while because they were a good lot. But they're all dead now and I'm still good for twenty years".

Mr. Brown is worried about the rising generation:
"There shouldn't be all this unemployment. This province will support any young fellow with enough backbone to get out and rustle. The secret is simply to get away from the crowd and start out alone in a new district. There's plenty of new land yet. The trouble is they all expect to live in luxury from the start".

Mr. Brown was one of the first sculling champions in B.C. He imported the first racing shell in 1896 from New York.

"When I got off the train I had to carry it 100 miles over rough country to Brown lake. It only weighed 32 pounds and a German helped me, but it was the toughest trip I ever made".

B.C.'s future is bright, Mr. Brown believes.

"The country itself is alright. There's gold in the mines and the land is fertile so nothing can ever keep us down".

Jim Brown published a small collection of his poems called "Prospectors Trail" in 1941. The introduction was written by long time friend Noel Robinson and marked "Christmas 1941".

Jim Brown passed away in Vancouver in January of 1942. His obituary mentioned that he was guide and Captain of the North Vancouver Rowing Club for many years and a close personal friend of the late Indian Poetess, Pauline Johnson. For many years he was a member of the Vancouver Pioneers' Association.

James Armes' youngest son Frank was the one who won the affection of the new school teacher, Doreen Pollitt. They were married in Vancouver on December 16th 1931.

In Vancouver, it seemed jobs were only available if you knew the right people or had political connections. So, the couple left for Dog Creek in the spring of 1932 and moved into the south end of Casa Grande. Placida Pigeon was living in the original log portion. With James gone, the couple spent the following winter at the Grandview Ranch with Ray and Chrissie Pigeon.

Employment for Frank was tenuous, a stint at logging for railroad ties and a Government contract for road maintenance between Dog Creek and Williams Lake were fill-ins. Frank stayed at the Moores' at Alkali Lake and would walk to Dog Creek to spend the weekends with Doreen and Bob.

**Frank and Doreen Armes with their first child, Bob. 1933.
Bob was born September 4th 1932.**

Although the Chinese had supposedly gleaned the last remnants of gold along the Fraser and mining was too much of an effort for "Whites", circumstances changed. The depression forced the locals to look for any source of income regardless of the effort required. The Armes family was no exception. Doreen wrote of this time in her Memory Journal;

"...In the mid thirties we were still in the depression, beef on the hoof was selling for five cents a pound. Believe it or not, one rancher acquaintance received,-not a cheque- for his fall shipment but a bill for shipping. Ranching is a once a year income occupation, and diversification is non-existent. The outlook was so bleak Frank's father decided to drop the ranch in favor of his other investments. We were left without a job, even without a home. It didn't take any persuasion for us to join Louie Krause and Frank Sakowtski in their placer mining of gravel along the Fraser River banks.

Very few ranchers could afford to hire extra help, not even at thirty dollars a month, bed and board supplied. George Thompson and Louis Krause had been ranch hands but now, unemployed they put their assets together and made their move. George spoke to Frank who hired Joe Dick with his team and wagon, Louis had a sturdy river boat and an outboard motor. It didn't take Joe Dick long to build grizzlies and load them on the wagon along with tents and camp supplies, long handled shovels, lengths of hose and a pump. There was a road from the gate at Alkali Lake to the banks of the Fraser and Louis had already tested for color, using the brand new gold pan.

Louis Krause with his pack, leaving Dog Creek to look for some color.

The hose poured water onto the grizzlies while Frank, George and Louis shoveled gravel into each. As the gravel was washed off, fine dirt and small rocks fell through. Gold, being heavier stayed on the mat. At days end our mats were washed in a tub of water and the fines moved to a gold pan and re-panned to wash off more of the gravel. Mercury was poured into the residue and stirred to gather the gold. The resulting lump was picked out and set on the red coals inside the door of the cookstove. The fire was out so there were no flames. The mercury burned off and you'd better be outside in the fresh air; mercury fumes are extremely poisonous. The resulting button was quite pure gold and sold at McKenzie's store for $29.00 an ounce".

The mining supplies for the summer of 1934 at the gate to Wynn Johnson's place at Alkali Lake.

Doreen wrote of the crews' arrival, set-up and baking on the river;

"By the time the boys got the grocery boxes onto the dry bar we had two of the tents up so I could start setting up the cook tent. The stove was necessarily small and light having no hot water tank and no oven. Oh yes, I did have an oven. It was one section of stove pipe, like this. There was an inner section to carry the smoke and outside that was a bulged part with a floor up and a door that opened to take two small loaf pans of bread. That bread baked well replacing store-bought quite adequately. When pots and pans and groceries were put away I was ready to throw myself on a bed, if there had been one there. Slim poplar posts with ropes secured crosswise and lengthwise completed the

bed frame and "springs". We had blankets enough for under and over. With lots of activity and plenty of fresh air sleep didn't have to be coaxed.

That was a good summer, satisfactory in more ways than one;- we were healthy and we were able to share our cash earned so that each of the four participants were able to find a winters' employment and settle ourselves into our new homes".

The summer of 1934.

Joe Dick's wagon with everything on the one load.

Louis Krause and Ada Place at the workings on the river.

Frank Sakowtski, (Mined with Frank and Doreen in 1934), Jim Worthington and Bert Erickson.

A.J. Drinkell wrote of the problems that the partnership with Charlie encountered during the depression;

"The gathering clouds of a nation-wide depression loomed forebodingly upon the horizon to finally burst overhead with chilling effect.

Cows could only be sold on a sluggish market for one-half cent per pound; consigned mostly to the processors of fox-feed. Even this market was lost when it was found the foxes preferred horse flesh. Top steers sold for three cents per pound if one could find a buyer.

Ranch wages plummeted to $20.00 per month, with board.

The value of merchandise depreciated in like proportion. We had by this time built up a very substantial stock, covering almost every line of merchandise, most of which was sold at considerable loss. Current bills however had to be paid, but with depreciated dollars. The situation was glum indeed.

Bankruptcy was the order of the day across the nation.

A newly appointed bank manager refused to extend to us our customary credit although we had quite recently wiped the slate clean....

While I struggled with the economic problems Charles and Ed (Hillman) worked like Trojans; the latter making no demands for wages other than to meet imperative needs....This combined effort eventually brought us through, somewhat battered by the downpour, but still in one piece".

Dog Creek Picnics.

PICNICS

A picnic was one of the most popular forms of socializing and an opportunity for the neighbors and families to get together. Pat Riley recalls that her Grandma, Theresa Pigeon, would rise at 4:00 a.m. in order to fry up the chicken and prepare the goodies for a day trip and picnic to Dog Creek Mountain. Another favorite picnic site was Mineral Springs.

The preceding pictures are of the Armes, Places, Pigeons and Meason families enjoying the break.

1934 and another new teacher, Sheila Doherty. This was the second school for Miss Doherty. She had taught in New Westminster at a small Roman Catholic School run by the Sisters of Saint Anne.

Dog Creek affected her profoundly, so much so that she eventually wrote two small books of her time there, "Deep Hollow Creek", written in the 30's and published in 1992, and "The Double Hook" published by New Canadian Library in 1989.

Anyone interested in the personalities, politics and sibling rivalries of the residents at the time, will find "Deep Hollow Creek" most informative. Although written as fiction the main characters are easily identified with their counterparts in real life.

Sheila originally boarded with Joe and Violet Place at the View Ranch but eventually moved out and rented a small cabin from Charlie. She stayed to teach the following year, 1935-36.

Sheila Doherty, Dog Creek teacher for 1934-1936.

**The Gang Ranch 1926.
Louis Seymour, Louis Tinmusket,
Walter Gaspard and Alec Raines.**

Walter Gaspard carried this well worn snapshot in his wallet until his death on March 20th 1995. It was taken with fellow cowboys on the Gang Ranch in 1926.

Louis Tinmusket was a native of Dog Creek and with his wife, listed on the 1911 census.

As well as working for the Gang he also worked for the McEwens and the Bishops at Empire Valley.

There is a small creek, Tinmusket, that runs into Dog Creek at the Gaspard Ranch that is probably named for the Tinmusket family.

Louis died at William's Lake on May 19th 1938 and was buried at Canoe Creek.

**Louis Tinmusket's funeral at the Canoe Creek Reserve.
May 1938.**

Note of Interest:
1) Eliza Mashue died on April 25th 1939, aged 48.
2) The Geographical Board of Canada changed the name of Little Dog Creek to Meason Creek on April 28th 1936.
3) Rita Margaret Hamilton was chosen as the "Williams Lake Stampede Queen" in 1935. Rita was later to become Hilary Place's wife.

**The 1933 Dog Creek Hockey team.
Front row-Charlie Place, Ray Pigeon and Geoff Place.
Back row-Third from left, Eric Hillman, fourth, Frank Armes.**

With no electricity, winter indoor activities were limited. No televisions or computers in Dog Creek. Outdoor activities were an opportunity to socialize with the neighbors and enjoy the exercise and possibly some friendly competition on the ice. Everyone got to participate.

Doreen Armes recalled her memories of skating at Dog creek:

"When I went to Dog Creek from Vancouver no one had skates and hadn't thought about skating. There was a lake up the hill behind the Gaspard and it certainly froze. I sent to Eatons for skates and so did several of the boys. Then Chrissie got going.

Back row- Ford Glasco, George Thompson, Norman Worthington, Ray Bill, Archie Sampson, Gilbert Harry, Hilary Place.
Front row- Ernie Glasco, Geoff Place, Ray Pigeon, Eric Hillman.
C - 1938

As soon as feeding was done on Sunday we took off for the lake or slough at the end of the ranch hayfields. It was just natural that the men had to have a hockey game. At the Mission School there was a hockey rink and a few of the native boys enjoyed that. A relative of Wynn Johnson's had played and begun to coach an Alkali Lake Ranch team made up entirely of natives. They called themselves the "Alkali Braves". They competed with Dog Creek, Springhouse and Williams Lake. Ruth Wynn Johnson, now Ruth Woodward's husband Billy got them smart uniforms and took them to Vancouver to compete against a Vancouver Allstars team. My dad, Fred Pollitt, Frank and I attended. The Alkali team played their hearts out.

In the two games they were defeated 1-0 and 2-1. They had a bit of a handicap in that the Vancouver rink was larger and they said the smokey air made them short of breath. (Also they were short of players for substitutions).

Diamond "S" blacksmith Joe Clemine played forward, he was a fast skater and an accurate shot. He was also a grandfather The announcer for the Vancouver game made a big thing of that. (Here comes the grandfather again)".

**Top – Charlie, Hilary and Geoff Place.
Bottom – Geoff Place and Unidentified player.**

1936 was the year young Davey Anderson arrived at the Gang Ranch. His father was the bookkeeper and storekeeper. No school existed at the time on the west side of the Fraser, so Davey headed to Dog Creek to attend school for the fall of 1937. He boarded at Charlie and Ada's place.

Miss Betty Webber was his teacher for the two school years 1937-1939. In 1940 Davey's parents followed to Dog Creek where they took up residence at Casey. Davey's mother was a nurse and in charge of any care that the natives required. The Indian Department supplied her with a medicine chest for this purpose.

**Dog Creek school C-1938.
Teacher, Miss Betty Webber, Evelyn Place, Placida (Paddy) Place, Jean Place, Wayne Place, Millie Place and Davey Anderson.**

Davey married Nora Rosette on June 22nd 1951. A son Philip arrived in 1952 and daughter Margarete in 1953.

Davey Anderson stayed on in Dog Creek after his schooling was complete.
These photos were taken by Alf Law, teacher in 47-48. They became close friends.

It was during this time that Drinkell took on the project of decorating and painting the Meason Ranch on Little Dog Creek that the David Spencer Ltd. department store, had recently purchased.

Mrs. and the "Colonel" Spencer.

The Gaspard Ranch was soon added, thus creating the Diamond "S" Ranch. The "Diamond S" was the Company logo for the department stores. David Spencer Ltd. had department stores in Victoria, Nanaimo, Vancouver, New Westminster and Chilliwack. The purpose for the entry into the cattle business was self interest. The ranching aspect of the Spencers' empire gave them total control of the supply and quality of beef to be shipped to their own stores.

Spencers purchased one thousand head of cattle in Alberta and had them shipped by rail to Agassiz, in the Fraser Valley.

In 1936 Frank Armes found his true vocation. He was hired by Colonel Victor Spencer as the Ranch Manager. Using Spencer's furniture delivery vans Frank and Dave Thompson loaded the cattle on the C.P.R. and shipped them to Ashcroft. They were met in Ashcroft with a chuckwagon from Dog creek handled by Pete and Maudie Louis. The slow moving cattle drive traveled in the early hours of the day before the traffic became heavy. This was the beginning of the Diamond "S" herd.

Doreen Armes described how the Spencers changed the outlook for the Dog Creek area in the thirties, this she classified as the high point:

"Colonel Victor Spencer (Spencer's store in Vancouver) took over the Gaspard Ranch-and eventually everything up Dog Creek-to develop the Diamond "S" Ranch. It, eventually ran over three thousand head of herefords. It became a model ranch, ecological use of range land, high percentage calf crop, prime beef cattle shipped to Vancouver to service Spencer's meat department".

Dave Thompson and Frank Armes at Little Dog.

THE 1940S

Frank, Doreen and son Bob moved into the newly painted Meason house at Little Dog Creek. Doreen described it "...*it was pretty posh....*". They lived there until 1938 when Frank felt that they should be closer to the center of operation and the family moved to the Gaspard.

Doreen wrote in January of 2003 of their stay at Gaspard:

"It moves me to think that the best part of my life was my time at the Gaspard Ranch when the children were young; Alan around two, Dot eleven years, Gordon twelve and a half, Bob seventeen. The ranch was productive; Spencer's stores took the beef, Harry Chamberlain and his family were very involved. Mrs. Chamberlain and Gladie were visitors each summer.

At the Dog Creek home on the Gaspard Ranch we entertained visitors from across Canada- and the English owners of the herd champion bull Sugwash Chieftain-etc....
He must have been proud to show off his ranch.

During the Second World War Colonel Victor brought guests to hunt, to fish etc...

The bird hunting was planned by Frank so as to take advantage of flocks on various lakes on Dog Creek Mountain. At each site there had to be one "gun" to walk around and "scare up" so the ducks or geese would fly over the hunters placed strategically behind a blind...

The kids in the Gaspard pool.

Colonel Spencer liked to have a whole mallard and roasted corn on the cob from our garden. Harry Chamberlain was always along, he looked after the Colonels liquor consumption.

I had Sarah Camille to help in the kitchen-at least until six p.m. when she had to go home. That got dinner ready but not cleaned up. My job alone. Coming back from hunting they had to have a shower, get into clean clothes, sit down and have a drink-then come to the table".

**A bird expedition on Dog Creek Mountain, 1938.
and a display of birds at Little Dog House.**

**Vic Spencer and Harry Chamberlain.
Harry Chamberlain was the Spencer employee
responsible for selecting the Beef for Spencer's stores.**

The Spencer children also spent time in the summer at the ranch. Ann the youngest, John two years older, Victor four years older than John and Barbara two years older than Vic.

The Armes family ran the Diamond "S" for Spencers until 1950 when Barbara Spencer took over, renaming it the Circle "S".

Vic Spencer with his first Pinto.

Vic, Anne and John Spencer.

Barbara Spencer on Vic's pinto and Liela Worthington at Gaspard.

More of the good life at Gaspard in the 40s.

Back row-Doreen Armes, June Worthington with Francis Worthington on shoulders, Ann Rose, Agnes Armes,
Middle row-Bob Armes, Jim Pigeon (baby), Chrissy Pigeon, Marie Pigeon, Theresa Pigeon, ?,
Front row-?, ?, Dorothy Armes, ?, Gordon Armes.

Above- Bob Armes, Dorothy Armes, Pete Tresierra, Gordon Armes.
Right-Gordon and Jimmy Oliver.

**Top-Frank Armes applying the
Diamond "S" brand.
Left-Marcel Bourgeois flanked by two
Unidentified friends.
Right-Harvey and Frank Armes.**

Officially the depression was over but supporting a family was still difficult. It was no different for Frank and Francis (Frankie) Place. The river ranch had only fifty acres of land that could be irrigated. Even though in the good years they could get three crops of alfalfa, it had been a struggle ever since the departure of J.S. and the failure of the transportation company.

Drinkell described the land;

"In exceptionally favorable years three crops would be cut.

Almost anything that grows in the ground flourishes there; watermelons, grapes, or peanuts".

The River Ranch, root cellar and old buildings as they were in the summer of 2005.

Frank and Frankie were raising three children, Wayne, Placida (Paddy) and Evelyn. He was mining across the river in January of 1940 when he collapsed and had to be carried up from the river via a very narrow trail. The terrain was so steep it required passing the stretcher from person to person in some sections. He died in William's Lake on the 25th of January 1940. The official diagnosis was a stomach ulcer with the contributing factor of a recent appendectomy. Frank was interred in the small cemetery behind the Dog Creek house, the only headstone marking the location.

Frankie and the children stayed until summer when Colonel Spencer added the farm to the Diamond "S". The Places then moved to Kamloops.

Left- Cousins, Millie and Evelyn.

Below-Paddy and Wayne in Kamloops.

The 40s, and Charlie and Ada were now full owners of the Dog Creek House. Drinkell covered the dissolution of the partnership;

"When Geoffrey was about to conclude his studies and with Hilary coming right along, the question of their future and the part they should play in the business became a lively issue.

Knowing how anxious mother was to have them remain near her, some planning for that eventuality was imperative.

They would undoubtedly, marry sooner or later.

If I withdrew from the partnership would it smooth the way for their full participation in the enterprise, and avert a repetition of the petty jealousies and strife which had once before beclouded the lives of this family?

Neither Charles or myself had any desire to terminate an arrangement that had been so amicable and satisfactory – the depression not withstanding – but the future demanded careful planning.

It was finally decided to dissolve the partnership with myself taking the store and Charles the remainder.

Co-operation did not end there however. I was to continue making my home with them and many mutually beneficial concessions were made throughout the years that followed".

Ada greeting a group in front of the Dog Creek House.

Ada continued to "hold court" in the big house. She had the assistance of hired native housekeepers as well as what she called her "Three Musketeers". Charlie was first, Ed Hillman second with Drinkell being the third. Drinkell wrote;

" The well being of her men-folk, whom she dubbed her "Three Musketeers", was second only to her concern for her two sons".

A.J. Drinkell, Ada and Charlie Place.

Gustaf Edvin Hillman (Ed) was second in command of the ranch and in charge when Charles was absent. Part of Ed's salary was room and board, thus entitling him to live in the main house with Charlie, Ada, and Drinkell. Ed had come to Dog Creek via a lengthy journey from New York in 1908, Seattle and eventually Ashcroft in 1912. He had worked on various ranches in the interior before settling in Dog Creek.

As Drinkell predicted the boys eventually married. Geoffrey married Gladys Williams from Horsefly. The marriage was short lived. Drinkell, who was on the front line probably had excellent insight as to the reasons;

"Meanwhile Geoffrey's marriage was not working out very well and Gladys left him to stay with relatives in Vancouver. It was not until their son was born (Courtney Allen) that Geoffrey learned of her pregnancy. His mother prevailed upon Gladys to return but no lasting reconciliation ensued.

Mrs. Charlie was very fond of Gladys and quite generous in many respects yet she seemed to get much of the blame for the estrangement.

It is possible that with the boys having played such an important role in her life the mother may have seemed too possessive to the young wife".

June 26th 1942 Hilary married the 1935 William's Lake Stampede Rodeo Queen, Rita Margaret Hamilton. They moved into Little Casey where they stayed for some years.

Drinkell wrote of Rita's distinguished heritage;

" It should be recorded that Rita is the daughter of Moffat Hamilton of Lac La Hache who in turn is a member of a very prolific family whose founder was one of the earliest of the Hudson's Bay Co. factors and an associate of their renowned fur trader, Peter Skene Ogden.

Hilary and Rita Place at Little Casey.

Her mother was the daughter of Augustine Boitano who, like, many others, found gold mining unprofitable.

He settled down to found a ranch and stopping house astraddle the Hudson's Bay Co. pack trail… He named it "Springhouse" due to the fact, so I am informed, that he tapped an underground spring while sinking a well in search of a water supply".

Trucking was the main source of income for brothers Geoff and Hilary during the early 40's, keeping the new airport on Dog Creek Mountain supplied.

Martin, Mrs. Eagle, Rita, Adrian, and Hilary Place.

In 1945 Rita and Hilary purchased the store from A.J. Drinkell, calling it "Rancher's Retail".

Far Left-Hilary Place at the Rancher's Retail Store.

Above-Dog Creek Main Street, 1948. The store is second building from right.

Ed Hillman laying the boards over the irrigation ditch across the road.

Hilary Place & Frank Armes leaving for jury duty in William's Lake.

Hilary Place in front of the main house.

Back-John Spencer, three unidentified friends, Vic Spencer.
Front-Colonel Vic Spencer and Harry Chamberlain.

Four days after Hilary and Rita's wedding, Joe and Violet's daughter Millie married Walter Olson in Kamloops on June 26th 1942.

Millie and Walter Olson.

War in Europe was raging and Walter signed up for the army. Millie returned to Dog Creek to live with her parents. Daughter, Lavina, was born on December 25th, 1942.

On Walter's discharge, the family moved to Salmon Arm. It was to be a short stay. Millie's mother Violet was stricken with leukemia and Millie and family returned to Dog Creek to help her parents during what became a prolonged illness.

**Right-Lavina Olson
at the View Ranch, 1943.**

**Below
A mustering out celebration
at the Palomar Supper Club
in Vancouver.
Back row-Wayne Place,
Evelyn Place, Robert
Johnson.
Front row-Paddy Place,
Victor Olson, Millie Olson
(nee Place), Walter Olson.
1946.**

After Violet passed away in 1949 Walter and family stayed on helping Joe before moving to Canim Lake in 1953. Now in 2007, Millie is still residing there.

Note of interest:
1) Placida Pigeon (nee Valenzuela) died at Casey February 5th 1942.
2) Marc Pigeon died in William's Lake February 23, 1947.

The railroader, Jasper (Jack) Fuoco and daughter Betty.

In May 1942 the Lakeview Hotel in William's Lake hired a new waitress, Betty Fuoco. Betty's family was originally from Revelstoke, her father, a railroader.

Geoffrey Place was driving the Dog Creek Stage picking up mail and supplies for delivery to Dog Creek. It was a short time after Betty's arrival that they met. Elizabeth (Betts) Carmella Fuoco and Geoffrey Place were married November 20th 1942.

They were living in William's Lake when their first child, a daughter, Denise Carmella, was born in 1944. Geoff was still driving the Stage Truck so the new family moved back to Dog Creek where Geoff also helped Charlie with the ranch. They lived in the small house that had been the old post office. The second child, a son Gregory Alfred, was born in 1945.

During the prewar years, Pan American Airlines flights from Seattle to Alaska would regularly pass over Dog Creek, thus the plateau on the mountain

Geoff, driver of the Stage, talking to Charlie, 1949.

Geoff with the locked mail bag.

was deemed an acceptable location for a refueling base. Ed Hillman was awarded the contract to supply the logs for the buildings and antenna poles. However, because of impending war clouds the charter was withdrawn.

The location was then taken over by the Royal Canadian Air Force. The building completed, it became designated as a staging unit and at its peak numbered around sixty men working three shifts a day.

"Off duty" on the mountain initially left little choice for entertainment and the enlisted men and officers spent many "off" hours at the Dog Creek House. Drinkell described this;

"Sing –songs around the piano were a popular pastime, during which that "Darling Clementine" and "the lady of many contrasting virtues, from Armetieres" received considerable attention. The uninitiated listening would be quite justified in thinking these two remarkable females, along with Maisie and Dozzy Doats,

were"domiciled in some place near Tipperary after bidding farewell to London's Leicester Square.

Poker games around the long kitchen table and dancing exercises in the lounge also helped to while away their off duty hours.

The coffee pot got worked overtime while the debates and arguments covered almost every subject under the sun....

... When their recreation hall was completed they were able to have a film show three times weekly which we were generously invited to attend'

Once monthly a dance was held to which local residents and a number of young ladies from William's Lake were invited".

The chef at the airport, Harry Tesch and staff, constructed *"A huge cake beautifully decorated and suitably inscribed"*. It was in honor of Ada's fifty-eighth birthday.

"She was overcome by the gifts and speeches but much more especially by the affectionate attention showered upon her by officers and men alike".

A.J. Drinkell being presented with the R.C.A.F. company crest.

The responsibility for the site was turned over to civilian control. The Department of Transport took over the operation. A.J. Drinkall took a contract with them to feed and board all the single men.

In 1946 and Betty and Geoff moved from Dog Creek to the Airport where Betty described her job as: *"chief cook and bottle washer. There were times when I was cooking for 21 men. We hired a girl, Hazel Johnson, from Springhouse to help with the children and peel a potato or two. I was a very busy lady 24-7"*.

Geoff and family moved to William's Lake in 1950 in order for the children to attend school.

**Some of the Place children, C-1948.
Corky, born July 10th 1942
Adrian, born February 5th 1943
Denise, born March 1st 1944
Gregory, Born August 27th 1945
Martin, born January 14th 1945.**

Winter at the airport.

This bear had to be disposed of for the safety of the children. It had been hanging around the cookhouse. (Betty Place)

The new recreation hall at the airport.

Dog Creek, like most other communities, sent their share of young people to represent Canada in World War Two. In Doreen Arme's Memory Journal she made note that Percy Pigeon was *"one of the "Dam Busters" in the Second World War"*.

Charlie and Jean Sealock, (nee- Place).

Victor and Anne Spencer.

Harold Armes in his uniform for the "Great War".

By 1947 the Dog Creek school board had been disbanded and their responsibilities fell to the William's Lake district. Among these was the selection of a teacher. September 1947, and the new teacher, Alfred (Alf) Law, arrived at the Lakeside Hotel in William's Lake. He had anticipated teaching at a school in William's Lake. Geoff Place picked him up and when he asked how far away the school was, the reply was *"about 57 miles"*, surprise!

Drinkell and the Places had always endeavored to select a teacher with a university education so were disappointed when they

Alfred Law, teacher for 1947-48 school year.

discovered Law was a Normal School graduate who had taught his first year in Kimberley. However, hindsight proves that William's Lake did much more than an adequate job in their selection.

Law was young, enthusiastic and athletic, a well received addition to Dog Creek. If present day respect for Alfred Law is any indication, he had a profound influence on the children of Dog Creek.

Alfred and Geoff arrived at the Dog Creek Hotel after dark and sat down to a late supper of what Alfred recalls was " *a very tough, but good, moose steak"*. The following morning breakfast was traditional "Cariboo". Alfred describes it:

"For breakfast we had bacon and eggs and some buttermilk pancakes. Pancakes alone have a long story. A crock was kept full of fermenting batter with more flour, salt,

etc. being added every few days as the basic mixture required. Great pancakes and nobody could remember when the batch started".

The new teacher boarded out at Little Casey with Hilary, Rita, and their two sons Martin and Adrian. He lived in the original log structure at the north end.

Alfred wrote;

"It didn't take long to meet the kids in the morning. Adrian and Martin were too young for school that year so everyone else was new to me. A load from the Diamond "S" brought in almost half of the kids while Rose and Violet Gaspard came from the rented house just west of the main house. I didn't find the house where Selena (Kalalest) and her four charges lived until a couple of weeks later".

Selina Kalalest, Stella and Mary Kalalest at the second Grist Mill.

The Kalalest family, Selena, Stella, Mary, Jimmy and cousin Antoine had recently moved from Alex's Gang Ranch homestead at the request of the social workers. They had insisted the children attend school and were given the choice of Big Creek or Dog Creek. The kids all started in grade one in the fall of 1947 and were living in the second grist mill building.

Alfred was an enthusiastic photographer and with his "Brownie" recorded many of the locals who he can name, each and every one, today. He also remains in touch with many of his former pupils.

The memorable sports day in Rabbit Park.
Back row-Antoine Kalalest, Mary Kalalest, Adeline (Dolly) Haller, Sherry Carlton, Wendy Worthington, Danny Carlton, Jimmy Kalalest.
Center row-Leonard Robbins, Curtis McNally, Dorothy Armes, Violet and Rose Gaspard.
Front-Stella Abel, Stella Kalalest, Marvin, Lavina Olson, ?, Lawrence Haller, Gordon Armes.

One of the most memorable events for the children was the organization of a "Sports Day" at the conclusion of the school year in June of 1948. It was the first and only, sports day the kids had known, and it remains in their memory as the highlight of that school year.

Alfred taught for only one year in Dog Creek then moved on to Alexis Creek the following year. He remains a fervent booster of Dog Creek and visits it on a regular basis.

It must have made an indelible impression!

Some of the girls in Alf's life in Dog Creek.

Clockwise from the top, Stella Abel, Rose Gaspard, Stella Kalalest, Mary Kalalest, Adeline Haller, Dorothy Armes, Alf and Sweet Cap. Center-Violet Gaspard.

And some of the men.

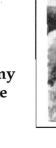

From the top-Lawrence Haller, Jimmy Kalalest, Gordon Armes, Augustine Charlie with Jimmy Kalalest and Antoine Kalalest.

Charlie Place, Alf Law and Ada Place.

1948 was the year of the great Fraser River flood. Irene Stangoe wrote in her William's Lake Tribune column "Looking Back" in December of 2005, she recalled an article written June 6th 1948;

"Saturday morning a twin-engine RCAF Dakota transport sat down on the local airfield and picked up so many sandbags that the big cargo plane "was stuffed like a turkey from end to end".... There wasn't even room to pick up the 3500 bags collected at Dog Creek Airport by Frank Armes of the Diamond "S" Ranch. A second plane was expected for this shipment. (Imagine – In Little Dog Creek!)".

Note of Interest;

    1) James Langman Armes died in Vancouver January 19th 1949.

       Maude Armes died September 28th 1968.

    2) Geoffrey and Betty Place's final addition to their family, Sylvia Charlene (Shawn), was born July 5th 1958.

    3) Frank and Doreen Armes' final addition to their family, Allan, was born April 4th 1947.

Raymond Saxie at Rancher's Retail.

Above-Mrs. Seymour with Saxie's new baby.

Right- Philomena and Marianne, on the Dog Creek House lawn.

THE 1950'S

The fifties had barely arrived and changes were in the wind. The war was over, prosperity and opportunities were available. Many of the older families had moved or were about to. The Measons were long gone, Walter and Elsie Gaspard were the last of their family to leave, going to William's Lake in 1948. Geoff Place and family had left the airport for William's Lake in 1951. Joe Place and family left in 1953 under what was the culmination of long family "strife" (as Drinkell referred to it) between Charles, Ada, Drinkell and Joe.

Walter and Millie Olsen (nee Place) also moved in 1953 to Canim Lake.

Ed Hillman pulled up stakes and left for Mission, B.C.

The reins of the Diamond "S" were turned over to Colonel Spencer's daughter Barbara. The Dog Creek holdings of the Diamond "S" were re-named the Circle "S". This change in management also initiated the change of ranch manager. Frank Armes and family left Dog Creek to manage the Nicola Lake ranch.

Barbara Spencer, the new boss at the Circle "S" Ranch.

Twenty four year old Kamloops boy Robert (Red) Allison arrived in Dog Creek on March 1st 1950. He had hired on as a cowboy for the Circle "S". His first home was a tent on Dog Creek Mountain, the site of George Wright's original sod roof cabin.

George Wright's cabin was being used as a cookhouse. Jossie Renaud and Barbara Copeland were the cooks for the cowboy crew.

Barbara Copeland's husband Bill had also been added to the Circle "S" crew.

Doug Cox in his book "Ranching, Now, Then and Way Back Then" describes the duties of the cooks in Barbara's own words;

"The breakfast menu was bacon and eggs, hotcakes and sausages, and some idiots even wanted porridge, plus gallons of coffee. The cowboys had lunch in the area in which they were riding, usually the Pigeon Ranch, and there was a man and his wife who cooked lunch for them. Suppertime back at the Dog Creek Cookhouse was a full meal, with pork chops or a roast and all the trimmings. The ranch had a garden but the cooks did not look after it. We were just too damn busy"!

Barbara and Jossie's day was described by Cox;

"Jossie and Barbara's started at 5:30 a.m. in the morning with lighting the cookstove fire and starting breakfast. They left the cookhouse at between 7:00 and 8:00

o'clock at night after the dishes were washed and dried. For this Barbara got paid $70.00 a month, plus the privilege of splitting wood and pumping water".

**Some of the cowboys who ate all that food.
Frank Teichrobe, Gilbert Harry, Bill Gardner, Tom Desmond,
Red Allison, Dale Lefferson, Antoine Harry and Philip Camille.
1952 at the Pigeon Ranch.**

Red Allison stayed with the Circle "S", becoming the cow boss in 1952. During his time in Dog Creek he met and married a William's Lake girl, Dionne Eagle, in February of 1954. Two boys, Bob and Gerry, were born on January 4th 1955 and May 31st 1956, respectively.

Barbara Spencer turned over the responsibility of the ranch to her brother Victor in 1958. Red and Dionne left Dog Creek and with a short diversion to the Okanagan, returned to the Gang Ranch where Red assumed the position of Cow Boss in 1959.

Tom Desmond, Red Allison and boss Barbara Spencer.

Barbara Spencer and Red Allison at Pigeon Ranch, 1950.

Dionne on "Patches" at Little Dog. 1954.

Lawrence Bruce and Red Allison at Gustafson Lake Cabin.

It wasn't all work, the above photo was marked "Let's Rodeo", June 12th 1951.

Dionne Allison at Little Dog Creek.

The main street of Dog Creek remained much the same: Charlie, Ada and Drinkell running the ranch and stopping house, with Hilary and Rita running the store and living in the apartment upstairs. Charlie passed away February 29th, 1956. He had spent his whole life in Dog Creek. This truly was the end of an era.

A book on Dog Creek would not be complete without a photo of the actual creek. Taken in 1948 with tool shed and the Dog Creek House upper left.

During the fifties Hilary and Rita had been renting the buildings from Charlie and Ada, but unable to come to a financial arrangement with his mother on the purchase of the store building, Hilary and family eventually moved on to William's Lake.

In the early fifties the ranch and stopping house actually became financially successful. Drinkell wrote of a trip to Vancouver on an annual shopping trip:

"They now owned outright over 3000 acres of land and around 300 head of cattle, plus the improvements, machinery and equipment--- a long, long stride from the 160 acre pre-emption and two cows.

It was a rich harvest well and truly earned through hard work, shrewdness and sheer guts.

Joyous as this moment was, another sweet taste of the fruits of their labor was accorded them when they called at their bank to arrange for the transfer of funds to Vancouver, prior to taking their annual holiday. They were nonplussed to receive instead a card stating that any cheque issued by them would be honored by the Canadian Bank of Commerce.

What richer harvest could they possibly reap"!

After the death of Charlie and with both her sons gone, it became progressively difficult for Ada to operate the ranch profitably. In September 1961 she sold the ranch to an American, George Demming, and moved to William's Lake where she stayed for a while with Rita and Hilary and then moved to live with Betty and Geoff.

Ada passed away in William's Lake August 28th, 1963.

Class of 1953 and the new schoolhouse, 1954.

The Armes family were not quite finished with Dog Creek as Doreen, with her son Allan, returned to teach for the school year 1953-1954. Dorothy and Gordon were finishing their education in Vancouver, living with their Pollitt grandparents. Dorothy wrote;

"The last time I was in the house (hotel) *was Christmas 1953. Mum was teaching school at Dog Creek that year. Dad was working at Miocene. Gordon and I were going to school in Vancouver (I hated it!). We had come up for the holidays and were invited for Christmas dinner. I don't remember too much about it except tiny Mrs. Place still intimidated me".*

After Frank's stint at the Nicola Lake Ranch they moved to Forest Grove. Doreen wrote in her Memory Journal;

"We went to Forest Grove where Frank and Bob logged, had a contract to cut railroad ties to ship to Britain. The whole concept was right outside Frank's experience and wasn't successful. He and Bob took a job in Khonk's Mill in William's Lake and I and Alan went to Dog Creek to teach.

Circle completed"!

*****

THE OLD SOURDOUGH

The cold of twilight settles on the hills
That darkly hide a camp, where by his fire
The sourdough pits his blaze against the chills
Of frost-sharp winds and ghosts of lost desire,
And sets atrail his dreams that never tire.

The lure of frontiers leads back to the past
When gold was bait for men in life's young glow;
Wild valleys hid rich veins where torrents cast
Their challenge to the souls who fought to know
The thrill of wealth, nor quailed, whate'er the foe.

Long-tried companions out of misty years
Take shape before dim eyes, enrich his dream
Their voices ring, their signals call he hears,
The clasp of hands, the smell of pipes would seem
To prove them real beneath the pale moon's beam

The dwindling campfire turns the ashes gray,
And slowly go the ghosts old memory keeps,
The friendly barks of dog-teams far away
Seem surety of transport when Time reaps.
Now, with his fire burned low, the sourdough sleeps.

James Nathaniel Jerome Brown

INDEX #1

Abel, Stella 165,166
Ah, Chong 43
Ah, Chun 43
Ah, Lee 45
Ah, Low Mr, & Mrs, 43
Ah, Moi 43
Ah, Pack 49
Ah, Tack 43
Ahzarez, Maria 21
Alexis, Chief 11
Allan, W. (Surveyor) 56
Allison, Bob 172
Allison, Dionne 174
Allison, Gerry 172
Allison, Red, 171,172,173,174
Anderson, Davey 21,138,139
Anderson, Margarete 138
Anderson, Philip 138
Angus, Dan 43
Antwyne, (Native) 90
Armes, Allan 142,177
Armes, Bob 125,142,146,177
Armes, Doreen 3,108,121,125,135,
141,142,146,162,177
Armes, Dorothy 142,146,165,166,177
Armes, Gordon 38,142,146,165,177
Armes, Frank 108,125,135 ,141,142
147,154,168,170,177
Armes, Harold 74,108,115,162
Armes, Harvey 108,147
Armes, James Langman & Maude
 66,107,119,125,169
Armes, Kathleen (Kitty) 108,115
Bacon, Chief Joe 78
Barnwell, Gladys 115
Basil, (Native) 79
Beaumont, Jane Ann 58
Big Louie 78
Billy, Willy 122
Bishop, Anthony 80
Bishop, John 80
Blenkhorns 101
Bob, French 10

Boitanio, Antonio 88
Boswell, 50
Bourgeois, Marcel 147
Bowe, Henri Otto 31
Boyd, Dr, Cecil 78
Boyle, Calvin 43,60,
Brown, Charles 14,40,
Brown, Henri 14
Brown, James Nathaniel Jerome
9,12,26,52,71,123,178
Brown, Samuel Leander Charles
8,14,43,58,93,123
Brown, William Mason 57
Bruce, Lawrence 174
Brundage, Mike 3
Bunnage, Bill 93
Burr, Joe 78
Byrues, George 43
Cahill, Earl 3
Camille, Sarah 143
Camille, Philip 172
Cargile, William 19,35,41,43
Carlton, Danny 165
Carlton, Sherry 165
Carmenaskat, 18
Caux, Jean (Cataline) 86,90,91
Chamberlain, Harry 142,143,154
Chelsea, F 46
Chevalier, Ted 82
Chew, Sat 78,79
Chinese Charlie, 66
Clemine, Joe 137
Clyne, Nora 117
Coldwell, Harry 97
Collin, Louis 16
Collin, Pierre 16,105
Collin, Peter 16,93
Conroy, Corporal J. 2,14
Cooney, Tom 53
Copeland, Barbara 171
Copeland, Bill 171
Cox, Doug 171
Coxon, Alice 57

Crang, Annie C. 27
Crazy Johnnie, 70
Cunningham, John 56
Cunningham, Ken 56
Douglas, Governor 5,58
Davis, Isaac 16
Davis, Jessie 15,39
Davis, John 15
Davis, Martin 15
Davis, Mary 15
Demming, George 176
Desmond, Tom 172,173
Dewdney, Edgar 22,39,46
Dick, Joe 126
Doering, Charles & Mary 96
Doherty, Sheila 132
Drinkell, A.J.
3,20,65,82,89,97,106,129, 109,113,119
140,150,151,158,159,163,175
Dunlevy, 51
Charlie, Augustine 167
Eagle, Dionne 172
Earle, Eric & Betty 115
Ellis, Thomas 62
Elwyn, Thomas 51
English, Benjamin F. 48,50
Eagle, Cecelia 153,
Erickson, Bert 129
Evans, Rufe 90
Fields, Silas 48
Fisset, Napoleon 56
Fook, Ah 90
Foster, F.W. 13,43
Frank, French 10
French, Robert 71
Fuoco, Betty 157
Fuoco, Jasper 157
Gagne, Pete 56
Gallagher, John 26,40,42,52,82
Gallagher, Nancy 42
Galpin, Thomas Dixon 60
Gardner, Bill 172
Gaspard, Barbara 122
Gaspard, Burt 122

Gaspard, Doreen 122
Gaspard, Edward 19
Gaspard, Felix 19
Gaspard, Frank 19,122,
Gaspard, Fred 19
Gaspard, Gordon 11,16,122
Gaspard, Isadore (Son) 19
Gaspard, Lillian 122
Gaspard, Matilda 18,19
Gaspard, Prosper 19
Gaspard, Rose 122,164,165,166
Gaspard, Violet 122,164,165,166
Gaspard, Walter 121,133,170
Gaspard, William 122
Gee, Chew 71
George, Le Po 65
Graham, Allan 23,25
Gunanoot, Simon Peter 90
Gustafson, Nils 56,71
Haller, Adeline (Dolly) 165,166
Haller, Lawrence 165,166
Hamilton, Gavin 90
Hamilton, Rita Margaret 135
Hancock, Ted 3
Hang, Chung 49
Harper, Jerome 23,24,67
Harper, Thadeus 23,48,67
Harry, Antoine 172
Harry, Gilbert 172
Haynes, 62
Hillman, Gustaf Edvin (Ed)
112,151,170
Hillman, Eric 135,153
Hinck, Elizabeth 94
Hing, Ah 78,80
Holden, William 106
Holland, Cuyler 60,62
Houpida, 14
How, Ah 78,80
Hymaben, Peter 90
Irving, Captain John 62
James, Helen 3
James, Lyle and Mary 3
Jane, John 40,41,43,46

Jarvis, Louis 56
Jennett, (Surveyor) 46
Johnson, Clara 104
Johnson, Hazel 160
Johnson, Robert 156
Kalalest, Alex 83,164
Kalalest, Annie 84
Kalalest, Antoine 164,165,167
Kalalest, Betsy 83
Kalalest, Jimmy 164,165,167
Kalalest, Mary 164,165,166
Kalalest, Metalan 84
Kalalest, Peter 84
Kalalest, Robbie 84
Kalalest, Selina 83,164
Kalalest, Stella 164,165,166
Kala'llst, Joe 84
Karnnatkwa, 16
Ko, Fouk 71
Kopmenak, 18
Krause, Louis 126,128
Kwonsenak, Matthilda 27,42(Note #1)
Laing, Frederick W. 10
Law, Alfred 3,140,163,165,167,168,
Lee, Sing 65
Lefferson, Dale 172
Leon, Blas 94
Leon, Serape 90,94
Lindley, Jo 5,6
Lindsay, Douglas & Doris 97
Lindsay, Francis Douglan 95
Lord, Alex 112
Loring, Alphonse 90
Louie, (Native) 79
Louis, Pete & Maudie 141
Lung, Wong 80
Lyne, Francis Opal 106
Lyne, Violet Ella 101
Lyne, William & Angelique 101
Manly, Sarah Ann 56
Marianne, 169
Marriott, Harry 27,93
Martin, G.B. 60

Mashue, Basil 121
Mashue, Eliza 121,135
Mashue, Elsie 120,122
Meason, Annie 31,32,33,89,114
Meason, Celestine 31
Meason, Eleanor Laing 31,89,114
Meason, Gilbert 31,52,75
Meason, Magnus 31,33,75
Meason, Malcolm Laing 21,31,33,75,
Meason, Theresa Laing 21,31,33,114
Meason, Theresa (nee Tuccatone) 114
Meason, William Laing 20,29,42,46,48,51,75,78,
Meason, William Laing Jr. 21,31,71
McDaniels, Dave 90
McGowan, Ned 92
McIntyre, Donald 48
McLuckie, Jack 32,89
McMillan, Jack 78
McNally, Curtis 165
Meiss, Matilda (nee-Gaspard) 87
Miller, (Mueller) John 63
Miller, John Jr. (Mueller) 63
Mondada, Stefano 88
Montgomery, 47
Moore, Corpelis (Dilly) 50,72,87
Moore, John E. 49,72,87,
Moore, Marie 87
Moore, Mrs. J.E. 72
Mootla, Margaret 17,19
Morrow, Charlie 28
Napoyet, Julia 63
Netherwood, Ada Halstead 100,
Oliver, Eric 117
Oliver, Jimmy 146
Olson, Lavina 155,156,165
Olson, Millie 149,155, 156,170
Olson, Victor 156
Olson, Walter 155, 156,170
Oppenheimers,16,27,35,41,82
Oppenheimer, Isaac 42
O'Shea, Michael John 21
Patenaude, Branwen 15

Patton, Tom S. 87
Peterson, Adelaid 21
Phair, Casper 78
Philipine, Simon 71
Philomena 169
Pigeon, Agnes 50,67,68
Pigeon, Chrissie 69,125,135,146
Pigeon, Claude 52,69,87
Pigeon, Jimmy 146
Pigeon, John Edgar 67
Pigeon, Louie 52
Pigeon, Marc 21,71,110,157
Pigeon, Marie 146
Pigeon, Moise 7,51,56,67,69
Pigeon, Percy 52
Pigeon, Peter 52
Pigeon, Pierre 52
Pigeon, Placida 125,157
Pigeon, Raymond 55,69,125,135
Pigeon, Rose 67,69
Pigeon, Teresa 67,68,146
Pigeon, Theresa (nee Philipine)
52,67,69,71
Place ,Ada 3,110,114,128,150,151,159
168
Place Adrian 153,160
Place, Alice 57
Place, Annie Elizabeth 59,72,95,96
Place, Betty 3,160,161,169,176
Place, Charles Riley 59,101,105,119,
137,150,151,153,158,168,175
Place, Courtney 151,160
Place, Denise Carmella 157,160
Place. Evelyn 138,148,149,156
Place, Frank 40,58,72,89,105,106,148
Place, Geoffrey 81,101,116, 117,135,
137,150,157,158,163,169,170,176
Place, George 57
Place, Gregory Alfred 157,160
Place, Harold 102,104,117
Place, Harry Beaumont 59
Place, Hilary 57,85,95,106,116,117,
137,150,154,164,175,176
Place, Jane 72,98,105

Place, Jean 102,104,117,138
Place, Joseph Smith Jr.
59,72,101,104, 105,119,132,170
Place, Joseph Smith
44,56,57,66,71,72,82,88,114
Place, Joyce 102
Place, Kathleen Ella 102, 104
Place, Martin 153,160
Place, Millie 102,117,138
Place, Placida 103,138,148,149,156
Place, Rita 153,164,175,176
Place, Sylvia Charlene 169
Place, Violet 155,156
Place, Wayne,138, 148,149,156,
Place, William 59
Pollitt, Doreen 115
Pollitt, Fred 136
Pow, Lim 81
Powell, Lieut. Col. 47
Prentice, James Douglas 61
Price, Miss Pansy 112
Pullet, Peter 13
Raines, Alec 133
Renaud, Jossie 171
Riley, Indian Commissioner 46
Riley, Patricia 53
Riske, L.W. 48
Rithet, R.P. 62
Robbin, Felix 86
Robbin, Moses 86
Robbin, Old (Native) 86,
Robbins, Leonard 165
Rose, Fred 34
Rosette, Nora 138
Ross, Ethel 106
Sakowtski, Frank 126,129
Saul, Isaac 40
Saul, Thomas 40
Scanlon, James Michael 89
Sealock, Charlie & Jean 162
Seymour, Louis 133
Seymour, Mrs. 169
Seymour, Raymond 169
Sim, Joy 65

Simone, Philipi 52
Simone, Theresa 51
Sing, Pack 49
Sing, Yam 5,35,39,43,65,71,
Skokum Joe 90
Smith, Dan 98
Smith, Joe 88
Soues, Charlie 37
Soues, Frederick 19,20,46
Spencer, Anne 144,145,162
Spencer, Barbara 144,145,170,172
173,
Spencer, John 144,145,154
Spencer, Mrs & Colonel
140,142,149,154
Spencer, Vic 144,145,154,162,172
Stangoe, Irene 168
Stupinfa, (Native) 52
Swannell, Frank Cyril 62,70
Tait, John R. 37
Takrwenack, 15
Teichrobe, Frank 172
Tesch, Harry 159
Thompson, Dave 141
Thompson, Family 109
Thompson, George 126
Thoresen, Ernie 27,64,88,90,91,94
Tinmusket, Louis 133
Tootsie, (Chief) 48
Tranq, Val 3
Tresierra, Alonzo 93
Tresierra, Pablo 88,90,91
Tresierra, Pete 117,146
Truan, Bud 56
Truan, Joe 56
Twentyman, Anthony 40,43
Twentyman, (Native)) 47
Unrau, Dorothy 3,38
Upton, Primrose 12
Valenzuela, Courision Margus 20
Valenzuela, Francesca 21
Valenzuela, Francisco 20
Valenzuela, Guadeloupe 21
Valenzuela, Jeannie 21

Valenzuela, Placida 20,87,110
Valenzuela, Rafael 20,44,57,64,82,87,
Valenzuela, William 21
Van Volkenberg, 62
Vaughn, William 90
Versepeuch, Isadore Conte de
Gaspard 10,19,71
Versepeuch, Antoine 11
Versepeuch, Ann Robert 11
Webber, Miss Betty 138
Wiggins, Dave 90
Williams, Gladys 151
Withrow, Samuel 48
Witte, sisters 84
Woodward, Billy 136
Worthington, Francis 146
Worthington, Jim 129
Worthington, June 146
Worthington, Liela 145
Worthington, Wendy 165
Wright, Bill 21,64,87
Wright, George 109,171
Wycott, Eva Frances 27
Wycott, James 27
Wycott, Maria 27
Wycott, Mary 27
Wycott, Tom (son) 27
Wycott, Tom (grandson) 28
Wycott, William Walter 26,40,71
Wynn-Johnson 88,98
Wynn-Johnson, Ruth 136

CONTRIBUTORS AND PHOTO CREDITS
The number designates the page number and the letter following, the position on the page if there is more than one picture. From left to right and top to bottom or clockwise from 12: o'clock.

Allison, Red and Dionne, 170, 171, 172, 173, 174.
Anderson, Davey
Armes, Doreen
B.C. Archives, 2, 8, 12, 22, 24, 39, 44,   61, 62, 70A, 70C, 85.
Cahill, Earl and Jocelyn, 63.
Chevalier, Ted
Chevalier, Zee
Clinton Museum, 6, 16, 20, 26, 56, 79, 80, 90, 91, 96A.
Drinkell, A.J.
Gaspard, Gordon, 121, 122, 133.
Hancox, Ida, 104C&D.
James, Lyle, Mary and Helen,41.
Kalalest, Mary
Kalalest, Stella, 83, 84, 164, 167D.
Law, Alfred, 98,105, 139, 163,165, 166, 167A,B,C&E, 168, 175.
Logan, Don, 23, 36, 37, 38, 55, 82, 88, 110, 148.
Olson, Millie, 96B, 102,103,104A,B, 117B, 138, 149, 155, 156, 162A.
Pigeon, Ray and Audrey,7, 51, 52.
Place, Betty,11, 45, 58, 59, 65, 72,74, 81, 87, 95, 97, 100, 101, 112, 116A, 117A, 118B, 119, 130A&D,132,134, 136,137, 150, 151, 153, 154A&B, 158, 159, 160, 161, 169.
Ratch, Betty, 94.
Riley, Patricia, 67, 68A, 69B&C.
Schreiber, Chris, 28.
Schreiber, John
Sworts, Bill, 10, 15, 18, 31, 123.
Tranq, Val and David,29, 32, 33, 34, 75, 76, 77, 130B,131B&C.
Unrau, Dorothy,17, 19, 30, 50, 54, 66, 68B, 69A , 70, 73, 74, 86, 99, 107, 108, 109, 111, 113, 115, 116B, 118A,C&D, 125, 126, 127,128, 129, 130C, 131A, 135, 140, 141, 142, 143, 144, 145, 146, 147, 154C, 157, 162B&C, 176.

INDEX #2
William's Lake Indian Agency 1911 Enumeration for Dog Creek Reserve #1

Name	Sex	Position	Relation	Age
Robin	Male	Head	Widowed	55
Robin Felix	Male	Son	Single	16
Robin Moses	Male	Son	Single	14
Kelest Alex	Male	Head	Married	28
Kelest Betsy	Female	Wife	Married	27
Kelest Peter	Male	Son	Single	11
Kelest Annie	Female	Daughter	Single	9
Lelest Metalan *	Female	Daughter	Single	8
Kelest Salearna*	Female	Daughter	Single	5
Sappie*	Female	Other	Widow	60
Matalan		Other	W	80
Camille	Male	Head	Married	40
Camille Agnes	Female	Wife	Married	32
Camille Mary	Female	Daughter	Single	12
Camille Celestine	Female	Daughter	Single	10
Camille Francis	Male	Son	Single	6
Camille Baby	Female	Daughter	Single	1
Tinmaskin Louis	Male	Head	Married	40
Tinmaskin Mrs.	Female	Wife	Married	32
Joe	Male	Head	Married	37
Joe Pauline	Female	Wife	Married	25
James Dick	Male	Head	Married	41
James Emma	Female	Wife	Married	29
James Pete	Male	Son	Single	18
James Elizabeth	Female	Daughter	Single	16
James Nancy	Female	Daughter	Single	11
James Madeline	Female	Daughter	Single	4
James Angela	Female	Daughter	Single	2
James Geotge	Male	Head	Married	39
James Catherine	Female	Wife	Married	19 ?
James David	Male	Son	Single	16
James Mary	Female	Daughter	Single	14
Joe Old	Male	Head	Married	75
Joe Sallas?	Female	Wife	Married	65
Charley	Male	Head	Married	65
Charley Sophia	Female	Wife	Married	51
Charley Isaac	Male	Son	Single	26
Charley Felix	Male	Son	Single	24
Charley Josephine	Female	Daughter	Single	17
Charley Harriet	Female	Daughter	Single	12

Charley White?	Male	Son	Single	5
Frank	Male	Head	Married	30
Frank Matalan	Female	Wife	Married	21
Frank Julia	Female	Daughter	Single	16
Phillip	Male	Head	Married	39
Phillip Millie	Female	Wife	Married	27
Phillip Maggie	Female	Daughter	Single	10
Phillip Eily?	Female	Daughter	Single	3
Jacky	Male	Head	Married	40

The * and ? denote writing that was not clear on the original documents.

BIBLIOGRAPHY

Armes, Doreen "Memory Journal" unpublished.

Bridge River, Lillooet News, Sept 24th 1936.

British Columbia, Its History, People, Commerce, Industries and Resources-
London 1912.

British Columbia Sessional Papers, Third Session, Fifth Parliament, 1889.

Brown, James Nathaniel Jerome, "Prospector's Trail" 1941.

Canadian Census, 1881, 1901, 1911.

Cox, Doug "Ranching, Now, Then and Way Back When" Skookum Publications.

Dewdney Trail, Frontier Publishing Ltd. Calgary, Alberta.

Drinkell, A.J. "Cariboo Chatalaine" unpublished biography of Ada Place.

Lindley, Jo "Three Years in the Cariboo" published by A. Rosenfield.

Lord, Alex "Alex Lord's British Columbia" Pioneers of British Columbia.

Marriott, Harry "Cariboo Cowboy " Gray's Publishing Sidney, B.C.

Patenaude, Branwen "Trails to Gold" Horsdal and Schubert.

Place, Hilary "Dog Creek, a Place in the Cariboo" Heritage House.

Secwepemc News, June 2002.

Watson, Sheila, "Deep Hollow Creek" McClelland & Stewart.

William Lake Tribune, Centennial Issue.

William's Directory 1895 Dog Creek.

Witte, Sisters "Chilcotin, Preserving Pioneer Memories", Heritage House.

*****

ISBN 142513637-0

9 781425 136376